WHAT SHOULD
MY CHILD
Read?

WHAT SHOULD
MY CHILD
Read?

SUSAN MOORE

AN ALBATROSS BOOK

© Susan Moore 1992

Published in Australia and New Zealand by
Albatross Books Pty Ltd
PO Box 320, Sutherland
NSW 2232, Australia
in the United States of America by
Albatross Books
PO Box 131, Claremont
CA 91711, USA
and in the United Kingdom by
Lion Publishing plc
Peter's Way, Sandy Lane West
Littlemore, Oxford OX4 5HG, England

First edition 1992

National Library of Australia
Cataloguing-in-Publication data

Susan Moore
What Should My Child Read?

ISBN 0 86760 041 1 (Albatross)
ISBN 0 7459 1703 8 (Lion)

1. Children's stories – Book-reviews.
2. Children – Books and reading. I. Title

028.162

Cover illustration: Michael Mucci
Printed and bound by the Book Printer, Victoria

Contents

Acknowledgements

OVER THE YEARS, MY EFFORTS to discover good books among the countless numbers being produced have been aided by the many prospective and practising teachers, in my own classes and in schools, who have recommended quality children's literature to me. Overseas readers, a close circle of friends at St Mark's Anglican Church, Malabar, Sydney, and my former colleagues on children's literature teams at the Sydney Institute of Education, especially Marian Henry, have also been extremely helpful.

Except for the most recent works on the market, there are no books listed here that haven't been read and loved by a great many children and by persons who have worked closely with children and with literature, and passed on some of their knowledge to me.

Also extremely helpful have been the presence of respected annual awards for children's literature in the United States, Britain and Australia, regular children's literature conferences and gatherings, and reliable children's literature journals. A majority of the books included in this guide have won major prizes or been included in national lists of notable books (see the prize lists on pp 161–165). Virtually all have been favourably reviewed in respected magazines such as *Horn Book* in Boston, or *Reading Time* or *Magpies* in Australia.

A number of the writers listed have also been accorded special recognition — the Hans Christian Andersen or Laura Ingalls Wilder Awards — for a lifetime's achievement. And many have visited our major cities to read from and speak about their work. Mollie Hunter's visit in the late seventies was, for me, particularly valuable.

Of the well-known writers and teachers who have not managed to reach Australia, I would particularly like to acknowledge Eleanor Cameron, whose letters over a long period have stimulated and encouraged me and whose painstaking criticism of the manuscript has saved me from some errors. Jerome Cushman's gifts of books and book lists were a great help to me when I was on study leave at the University of California in 1980. The staff of the *School Magazine* in New South Wales, especially Megan McDonald, have also provided continuing support and advice and have introduced me to many knowledgeable people in the field.

Nancy Shearer, the former owner of Shearer's Book Store, and Robin Morrow of the Beecroft Children's Bookshop have recommended countless good books. Denise Hoeflake of the Tangara School, Elizabeth Maher of the City of Sydney Library, and the children's librarians at the Waverley and Pagewood municipal libraries have given me access to materials I would otherwise have taken weeks and months to find. Karen Jameyson has scrutinised my final lists and offered suggestions for improvement, with a knowledge far greater than mine.

Finally, for their maturity of judgment, their devotion to the writers we read together and their encouraging comments during a key period in my own professional development, I want to acknowledge my first full-time fourth-year children's literature class at the Sydney Institute of Education: David Allison, Maria Allison, Laurie Ang, Branka Badel, Vaseljka Borojevic and Rae Scott. For their loving interest in children's books and their eagerness to share my involvement in them, I must thank my friends Helen Pinnock, Sandy Gaskin, Anne Lawrence, Charlotte Clutterbuck and Mary Rose Pintado. For her help with the illustrations, I'm indebted to Caroline Cox. And for their excellent editorial suggestions and encouragement, I am grateful to Ken Goodlet and John Waterhouse of Albatross Books.

Preface

THIS BOOK IS FOR PARENTS eager to find good literature for their children, but uncertain about where to start. The revolution in children's literature responsible for the presence of hundreds of new novels for eight- to fifteen-year-olds has made it increasingly difficult for well-intentioned adults to know which authors and which individual works are best.

What Should My Child Read? offers a wide range of suggestions for parents whose children are starting to read seriously and looking for stimulating material. Books from many parts of the world, but especially Australia, the United States and the United Kingdom, have been chosen for their appeal and readability, the quality of their language, their imaginative depth and their balanced approach to life.

Excluded are books that are crass or nihilistic, schmalzy or slick. Over the past forty years, so many excellent novels have been expressly written for children that there is little justification for recommending works unlikely to have enduring value. In the belief that most parents want their children to read books that are nourishing as well as entertaining, I have chosen novels capable of enlarging young readers' experience in a way that does full justice to their capacity for wonder. I have avoided those children's books that represent assaults upon innocence — a feature of the vast change in public taste — against which I have reacted strongly.

Good novels increase children's understanding of themselves, others and the universe without being demoralising or, worse, destabilising. This is not to suggest that children should be protected from every book that might cause embarrassment, discomfort or pain. First-rate literature for people in every age group has always rendered a broad range of painful, as well as pleasurable, experience. Such potentially upsetting subjects as sudden or premature death, serious injury or handicap and adult brutality have long been treated in books for children.

Although there are subjects most of us would consider inappropriate for children's literature — for instance, incest, multiple murder, rape, unrelieved terrorism and organised crime — topics once considered wholly unsuitable are now being tackled by widely respected authors. In the hands of gifted writers for adolescents, such commonplace contemporary disorders as mental unbalance within the family, parental neglect of children and street crime are handled with a firm and balanced understanding of their place in the total scheme of things.

Even a theme as potentially sensational as the suffering of four children abandoned by their crazed mother in a parking lot (the subject of Cynthia Voigt's fine novel *Homecoming*) can be confronted with admirable soundness of judgment, provided that a writer's grasp of the whole of experience is securely based.

The essential difference between the good books and the bad is a difference in the point of view — moral and linguistic — of the author. Those novels which treat both traditionally acceptable topics and once-forbidden ones, if they are worth reading, avoid sentimentality and sensationalism. Unlike third-rate practitioners whose sales sometimes skyrocket, the better novelists shun fundamental distortions of experience, addressing controversial issues in their entirety rather than in their more loaded aspects.

A common view of literature in our post-modernist age is that unless it concentrates on the ugly, the bleak and the grim, it isn't 'real' but a cop-out, the product of a stubborn refusal to see things as they are. This is a basic misunderstanding of the nature of the most valuable imaginative writing. Essential to all of the best literature for children and adults is a sense of proportion. Gifted children's writers (like gifted adult ones) show their respect for reality by rendering it in all its fullness, neither leaving out pain nor exaggerating its importance. A feature of their understanding of what young readers can accommodate emotionally is the recognition that portraits of the things that hurt need to be balanced by a powerful rendering of the sources of joy and delight.

When the distinguished American writer Katherine Paterson spoke to a packed hall of parents, teachers, writers and children in Sydney in 1988, one of her more memorable actions was to distinguish her own fiction — grounded in a Christian view of the kingdom of God — from that species of literature, so popular everywhere, which offers readers phantom pleasures but no real hope. In the process, she made it perfectly clear that the traditional literary values which we associate with the works of the greatest writers — Dickens, for example, or Hopkins — apply as much to children's as to adult writing. All major literature, she said, is marked by a wholeness of vision which doesn't minimise real difficulty, but which knows the meaning of promise.

Many readers — both children and adults — cry in pain at the end of Katherine Paterson's two most popular novels, *The Great Gilly Hopkins* and *Bridge to Terabithia*. But it is a rare reader who finishes either book without feeling consoled and enlarged. The humour and charm of many of the events portrayed balance the suffering so effectively that a feeling of spaciousness ultimately prevails, and the reading audience feels released. To enlarge their readers' sense of possibility, the greatest children's novelists — like the greatest adult ones — affirm the worthwhileness of life at the same time that they look unflinchingly at some of its most costly features.

In a discussion of the nature of artistic achievement, the American Southern writer Flannery O'Connor once remarked that 'the roots of the eye are in the heart'. Mediocre writers are never distinguished by their unusual powers of observation or their generosity of spirit. Their books are flat and inert — without resonance, density or weight. They lack the power to lift readers beyond themselves.

One of the more striking qualities of book after book included in this guide is their emotional acuteness. The authorial voices we hear have authority, because the persons behind the prose are deeply in touch with their own feelings and the feelings of others. As a result, they inspire confidence and trust. In their company, we know where we are.

*   *   *

In this book I have not recommended classics familiar to just about everybody, or novels written for adults but suitable for older children. Books such as the *Anne of Green Gables* series, *Black Beauty*, *The Wizard of Oz*, *Wind in the Willows*, the *Princess and the Goblin* series, all the *Winnie the Pooh* books, *Watership Down*, *The Hobbit*, *To Kill a Mockingbird* and *Lord of the Flies* are not listed and described, because it is lesser known works of more debatable status which parents regularly ask about.

Books by acclaimed writers which are difficult to obtain, such as Anne McCaffrey's fantasies, have also been omitted. With the exception of some novelists just starting out, only those whose volume of work is substantial have been included.

Overall, I have tried to perform a service for parents similar to the one performed by the best librarians and children's bookstore owners, by answering the questions most often asked of them: What do you have for a ten-year-old boy who is interested in the outdoors? Or a thirteen-year-old girl wanting to know more about the complex demands of family life? Or a child who insists on being amused or held in suspense?

Are there authors who have written a series about the same child or the same group of children? Can you recommend a novel or novels about ordinary children facing ordinary difficulties? Have you anything on outer space, time travel, great heroic struggles against the elements, monsters or tyrants?

To make things easier for readers to find exactly what they are looking for, this book is divided into two main sections: *Books for younger readers* and *Books for older readers*. These divisions correspond with the library designations 'Junior Fiction' and 'Teenage Fiction'. For each title a suggested age range, intended as a rough guide but no more, is given.

Some children, and some books, defy all adult predictions about what is most suitable for whom. My advice to parents is to encourage youngsters to browse among recommended novels. If some don't appeal at all, for whatever reason, they should be put aside in favour of others. Very able readers will probably love almost everything listed; average readers' reactions will be much more variable.

Under the large heading 'Realism' (books about ordinary life) and the almost-as-large heading 'Fantasy', novels for readers eight to twelve are listed under the most common and most requested topics currently available. For twelve-to fifteen-year-olds, the large divisions (Realism and Fantasy) are the same, but the subdivisions are slightly different because of the difference in maturity of the children concerned. Novels for intermediate readers in the eleven to thirteen age group are included in the *Books for younger readers* section.

A few excellent works, based on real events which employ many of the techniques found in novels, appear even though they are non-fiction. Their non-fiction status is indicated. Lists of major prize winners for the past thirty years can be found in the concluding section. Prolific or unusually gifted authors who have produced first-rate books for different age groups or in different genres such as simple realism, historical fiction and fantasy are cross-referenced. Indications of where the book can be most readily acquired are provided throughout the guide. The editions most easily obtained in Australia and the UK are, in general, the ones listed, but the publication dates given are normally first edition dates. Under each entry, additional books by the same author are recommended.

Books I consider outstanding under each topic area are starred (*). But I can't pretend that my tastes are everybody's. Although most devotees of children's literature would agree that *A Wizard of Earthsea*, *Tuck Everlasting* and *Roll of Thunder, Hear My Cry* deserve to be starred, opinion about dozens of other novels is divided. I have tried to indicate through what I say about starred entries why I have such a high regard for them. All are books that deserve to be re-read many times.

I have indicated the possible availability of recommended books in the following way under each entry:

LIBRARY means likely to be found at libraries.
CHILD   means likely to be found in paperback at children's bookshops.
GENERAL means likely to be found in paperback at general bookshops.

Inevitably, because of the volume of fine books in print, works and writers unknown to me and to my many advisers will have been omitted unwittingly from all lists. A future update of the guide will, I hope, rectify omissions and errors discovered by readers and brought to our attention.

Part A

Part A

Books for younger readers (8 to 12 years)

REALISM:
*Family life/
School/Friendship*

'Stories are old the way human biology is old. No matter how much they have produced in the past in the way of fruitful inspirations, they are never exhausted.

The story of Christ. . . can never be diminished by the seemingly infinite mass of theological agonizing and insipid homilies which have attempted to translate it into something more manageable. It remains, like any other genuine story, irreducible. . . like the body of a new-born child.'

Ted Hughes, 'Myth and Education'

SINGLE NOVELS

☞ *The Summer of the Swans

Betsy Byars, illustrated by Ted McConis, Avon, 1970
(USA). Newbery Medal, 1970. Ages 10-12 years.
LIBRARY, CHILD, GENERAL

Fourteen-year-old Sara Godfrey's struggles with her retarded brother Charlie, her beautiful older sister and the aunt who cares for the family, Willie, are sensitively handled in one of the most accomplished of Betsy Byars' many fine books. Notably strong are Byars' rendering of Charlie, of Sara's concern when he disappears in the forest near their home and of Sara's developing friendship with a boy she's wrongly distrusted, Joe Melby, who helps her to find her brother.

Other titles: *The Pinballs, The Not-Just-Anybody Family* (see p. 47) and many others.

☞ *M.E. and Morton

Sylvia Cassedy, Crowell, 1987 (USA). Ages 11-13 years.
LIBRARY

Sylvia Cassedy is unusually adept at depicting the reactions of highly vulnerable and lonely children to adult ineptitude and insensitivity, as the reception accorded her first novel, *Behind the Attic Wall*, demonstrates. In *M.E. and Morton*, she traces the growth in awareness of a sixth class child named Mary Ella — M.E. — whose friendship with a new girl, Polly, gradually changes her attitude towards her retarded brother, Morton, her parents and herself.

Cassedy's handling of M.E.'s gradual movement away from conventional egotism into a more generous responsiveness to her brother is delicate and true, as is her rendering of limitation in M.E.'s parents and of the sometimes extreme means Mary Ella has to adopt to alter a rigidly restrictive family dynamic.

Other titles: So far in Australia, *Behind the Attic Wall* (winner of numerous awards including an IRA–CBC Children's Choice award).

☞ *The Present Takers

Aidan Chambers, Magnet, 1983 (England). Ages 10-12 years. LIBRARY, CHILD

This account of brutality in the school playground and its environs is very effective, both because it gets right all of the subtle and not so subtle forms of cruelty practised by insensitive children and their parents, and because its solution to the apparently intractable problems it poses is imaginative and wholly credible. On the helplessness of well-intentioned but distant adults, and the flexibility of two bright and vulnerable sixth class pupils, Chambers is particularly convincing. As in *Seal Secret*, he enlists enormous sympathy for every living creature hurt, brutally threatened or demeaned by others.

Other titles: *Seal Secret*. Chambers' books for older children, including *Now I Know* (Bodley Head, 1987), a flawed, experimental novel about a group of young people who relive aspects of the crucifixion of Jesus as they film modern violence, are less successful. Some are also controversial because of their sexual explicitness.

☞ Dear Mr Henshaw

Beverly Cleary, illustrated by Paul O. Zelinsky, Puffin, 1983 (USA). Newbery Medal, 1984. Ages 10-12 years. LIBRARY, CHILD, GENERAL

Although Beverly Cleary relies on diary narration, which in lesser writers often issues in a static plot, she manages to invest Leigh Botts' introduction to the joys and difficulties of writing with vitality and punch. Leigh's life at home, his friendships, his love for his estranged father and his bond with his dog Bandit (whom his father has taken) come entirely alive as he writes about them to an admired fellow writer, Boyd Henshaw, who won't let him get away with any form of verbal looseness.

Other titles: *Ribsy* (see p. 39), *Ramona the Pest* (see p. 47) and many others.

☞ The Village by the Sea
Paula Fox, Orchard, 1988 (USA). Boston Globe-Horn Book Award, 1989, Hans Christian Andersen Medal winner. Ages 10-13 years. LIBRARY

When her father has a heart bypass operation, ten-year-old Emma goes to Peconic Bay to stay in a huge ocean house with his estranged and egocentric sister Bea and her beleaguered husband Crispin. How she copes for two weeks, away from her parents, uncertain about whether her father will live, with nobody her own age — at first — to talk to, is Paula Fox's subject, subtly and sparingly handled.

Here, as in Fox's other fiction, interest is sustained by the strength of her depiction of the world built by an isolated child in the face of adversity. Descriptions of the Long Island coast, Aunt Bea's morbidly selfish behaviour and Uncle Crispin's attempts to handle it, and Emma's insights into others are masterful.

Other titles: *How Many Miles to Babylon?*, *One-Eyed Cat* (see p. 106) and many others.

☞ I Am Susannah
Libby Gleeson, Angus and Robertson, 1987 (Australia). Ages 10-13 years. LIBRARY, CHILD, GENERAL

Although Gleeson's style tends towards flatness, the worlds she creates are believable. In this novel about a young girl's loneliness in Sydney following the departure of her best friend to Melbourne, apparently mundane events — especially, Susie's encounter with an artist whom she has dubbed the Blue Lady — turn out to be more interesting and beneficial than they seem at first.

Nothing in this book works as well as the parts of *Eleanor, Elizabeth* which take its heroine back to an earlier day; but the relationship of a hard-working single mother and her daughter is nicely managed.
Other titles: *Eleanor, Elizabeth*.

☞ *Get On Out of Here, Philip Hall

Bette Greene, Dial, 1981 (USA). Ages 10-12 years.
LIBRARY

Beth Lambert gets the stuffing knocked out of her on two public occasions at which many of the black folk in her home town of Pocahontas, Arkansas, are gathered. Thinking a leadership prize is going to be awarded to her, she stands up expectantly and is howled down when it goes to her chief rival, Philip Hall. Barely recovered, in a major race between the Pretty Pennies and the Tiger Hunters, she throws her baton instead of passing it and of course loses the race for her team. In disgrace, and deposed as leader of the Pennies, she decides to leave town and live with her grandmother.

With characteristic humour, warmth and astuteness, Bette Greene dramatises Beth's ensuing struggle. As well as creating a wonderfully robust and endearing heroine, she evokes, from the inside, a way of life. This is the more remarkable — as the Newbery Honor award implies — because she herself is white.
Other titles: *Philip Hall Likes Me, I Reckon Maybe* (a prequel), *Summer of My German Soldier* (for older readers) and others.

☞ Elvis and His Secret

Maria Gripe, illustrated by Harold Gripe, Dell, 1972 (Sweden). Hans Christian Andersen Medal Winner. Ages 10-11 years. LIBRARY

The brutality of Elvis Karlsson's parents, who berate him for being uninterested in conventional pursuits and neglect him out of an inveterate selfishness, is balanced in this unusual book by Gripe's portraits of other sensitive adults — notably, a young man named Peter who looks after Elvis's friend, Julia, and Elvis's

Grandad. Of course, most of us have known parents who throw cold water on a child's pleasures and fail to appreciate their offspring's real virtues. But it is a rare writer who dares to portray such parents in a book for upper primary school children — and, at the same time, to allow a very interesting and loving child to develop fully in spite of them.

Other titles: *Julia's House, Hugo and Josephine* and others.

☞ Boss of the Pool

Robin Klein, illustrated by Helen Panagopoulos, Omnibus-Puffin, 1986 (Australia). Ages 10-12 years.
LIBRARY, CHILD, GENERAL

Although Robin Klein's books seem to me overrated, this short novel is convincing and balanced in its handling of difficulty. Very gradually, Shelley Treloar discovers that her hard-working mother and a retarded boy at the Home where she's employed have more to be said for them than is immediately apparent. On forms of selfishness in young people like Shelley, and ways of overcoming them, Klein is pointed and accurate.

Other titles: *Penny Pollard's Letters* (see p. 48), *Hating Alison Ashley* and others.

☞ Mama's Going to Buy You a Mockingbird

Jean Little, Puffin, 1984 (Canada). Canadian Children's Book of the Year, 1985. Ages 10-12 years. LIBRARY

Although death is no longer a taboo subject for children's books, the slow wasting away of a parent is a subject few writers for intermediate readers would dare to attempt. Jean Little manages it quite well, dramatising the effects on young Jeremy of the growing realisation that his father isn't going to recover from the operation he has had in the

city, away from his children. Jeremy is helped in his lonely struggle by his friendship with a girl at his new school, Tess, who shares his delight in books, big words and racing along windy streets, and confides in him about her spotty family background.

Other titles: *Kate, Listen for the Singing* and others.

☞ *Sarah, Plain and Tall

Patricia MacLachlan, illustrated by Vanessa Julian-Ottie, Harper, 1985 (USA). Newbery Medal, 1986. Ages 8-10 years. LIBRARY, CHILD, GENERAL

A charming tale based on an actual event in Patricia MacLachlan's family history, *Sarah, Plain and Tall* details the changes that take place in the lives of Caleb and Anna on a farm in the Midwest when a young woman from Maine answers their father's mail order advertisement for a wife. MacLachlan's style and timing are impeccable. She is unusually skilled at illuminating apparently innocuous but significant features of rural life in unconventional family settings.

Other titles: *Arthur, For the Very First Time, Cassie Binegar* and others.

☞ *Handles

Jan Mark, illustrated by David Parkins, Puffin, 1978 (England). Ages 10-12 years.
LIBRARY, CHILD, GENERAL

Sent by her mother to the country for a 'holiday' with her brusque aunt and uncle and their nasty, spoiled son Robert, Erica Timperley survives by delivering her aunt's home-grown vegetables by bicycle to a small industrial estate. At its heart is a repair shop run by three characters whose unlikely names ('handles') are 'The Gremlin', 'Bunny', and 'Elsie'. There, without her relatives' knowledge, she spends most of her time learning about her passion, motor bikes. Jan Mark describes Erica's unusual summer with an understated sympathy, wit and restraint which intrigues reluctant, as well as seasoned, readers. She is particularly good at depicting strategies deployed by venturesome children

temporarily trapped by rigid, maddening constraints.
Other titles: *Thunder and Lightnings* (Carnegie Medal,
1976), *Under the Autumn Garden* and many others.

☞ The Jetty

Christobel Mattingley, illustrated by Gavin Rowe,
Hodder and Stoughton, 1978 (Australia). Ages 10-11
years. LIBRARY

In her novels for young readers,
Christobel Mattingley portrays
ordinary Australian children
battling for self-respect in
run-of-the mill surroundings,
especially small country towns.
The protagonist of *The Jetty*, Brad, is not an exception to
this general rule. After his father drowns, Brad's hatred
of the jetty which represents Kanbi Bay's livelihood
increases. When a storm endangers the jetty's position,
Brad hopes that it will finally fall to bits. But this
doesn't happen. Instead, Ian Fergus, sent by Adelaide
authorities to test the jetty's soundness, changes Brad's
attitude towards the sea, its fish and the jetty itself.
Characteristically in Mattingley's books, this change
occurs in a natural, understated, persuasive way.
Other titles: *Tiger's Milk, Windmill at Magpie Creek* and
others.

☞ Henry's Leg

Ann Pilling, illustrated by Rowan Clifford, Kestrel, 1985
(England). Guardian Award, 1986. Ages 10-12 years.
LIBRARY

Eleven-year-old Henry Hooper's life is fairly chaotic
after his father leaves to set up house with a younger
woman. In between starting and leaving one typing
job after another, his mother makes half-hearted
attempts to keep their large old home in order. She
finds this especially difficult, because Henry collects all
sorts of weird and wonderful things: a tobacco tin full
of old coins, a broken air rifle, a snap-box used as a
lunchbox in a mine, wire coat-hangers, a gas mask and

dead hedgehogs (which he moves to a neighbour's freezer). One of his finds, a store dummy's leg, turns out to be a repository for stolen jewels; and the parts of the novel that aren't focussed on Henry's daily round depict the difficulties he has in protecting the leg. . . and himself.

As in her other fiction, Ann Pilling is amusing and authentic on the feel of her characters' existence. She is very good at blending mystery and studies of family life.
Other titles: *On the Lion's Side*, *The Year of the Worm* and others.

☞ Family at the Lookout
Noreen Shelley, illustrated by Robert Micklewright,
Oxford, 1972 (Australia). Australian Children's Book of
the Year, 1973. Ages 10-12 years. LIBRARY

The Lookout is a twenty-five room house at Gully Heights in the Blue Mountains inherited by the Wetherall family when Mr Wetherall's great-uncle Joseph, an eminent ornithologist, dies. Moving into the area from a Melbourne flat changes their lives completely. Through the eyes of Mark, the oldest of the three Metherell children, we get to know Gully Heights: the land, the house and local inhabitants, including a mysterious near neighbour, the prickly and strange Miss Hatch. A mystery surrounding Miss Hatch and great-uncle Joseph is resolved only after a vividly described bushfire threatens everyone in the vicinity. The novel is an adept and faithful chronicle of everyday life in the Blue Mountains.
Other titles: *The Other Side of the World*, *Cat on Hot Bricks* and others.

☞ A Taste of Blackberries
Doris Buchanan Smith, illustrated by Caroline Binch,
Puffin, 1975 (USA). Ages 8-10 years. LIBRARY, CHILD

When young Jamie Mullins is fatally stung by a bee, his best friend — the unnamed narrator of Doris Buchanan Smith's first book — is shocked beyond his years. With admirable tact and candour, Mrs Smith dramatises the immediate effects of Jamie's death on this child and others close to him as they move beyond shock into acceptance. No other novel for eight-to-ten-year-olds that I have read handles this difficult subject with greater sensitivity or sense.

Other titles: *Laura Upside-Down*, *The First Hard Times* and others.

☞ *Gaffer Samson's Luck

Jill Paton Walsh, illustrated by Brock Cole, Puffin, 1985 (England). Grand Prix winner of the Smarties Prize. Ages 10-12 years. LIBRARY, CHILD, GENERAL

With the possible exception of *A Parcel of Patterns*, this seems to me the best of Jill Paton Walsh's books. It describes the world entered by young James when his father changes jobs and moves the family from the Yorkshire hills to the flat village fenland considered enemy territory by the toughest children at his new school. The immediate saving feature of James's new life is his friendship with an elderly neighbour, Gaffer Samson. Eventually, however, other things help him out in exciting and unpredictable ways. Walsh is especially skilled at contrasting the ritual behaviour of young louts with the old-fashioned civility of a man who knows what 'pickyness' means in the daily round of a boy.

Other titles: *Fireweed*, *A Parcel of Patterns* (see p. 135) and many others.

☞ Five Times Dizzy

Nadia Wheatley, illustrated by Neil Phillips, Oxford, 1982 (Australia). Ages 10-12 years. LIBRARY, CHILD

The flavour of life in inner city Sydney — Newtown — is nicely caught in Nadia Wheatley's cheerful, funny book about one Greek family. Mareka's struggles with children in her neighbourhood, her efforts to aid her lonely and dislocated grandmother (Yaya), her ups and downs in the milkbar owned by her parents, and her brainstorms are all colourfully treated. The novel's illustrations by Neil Phillips are especially good.

Other titles: *Dancing in the Anzac Deli* (sequel) and

others, including an outstanding picture book for middle primary children, *My Place*, illustrated by Donna Rawlins.

SERIES

☞ That Julia Redfern
Eleanor Cameron, illustrated by Gail Owens, Dutton, 1982 (USA). Ages 9-11 years. LIBRARY

This series, available at present only in part and at some libraries, will appeal most strongly to highly imaginative children. For Julia is a budding writer, full of ideas which make perfect sense to persons with expressive gifts, even though they seem strange to those with conventional minds, like Julia's rather obtuse Aunt Alex. In *That Julia Redfern*, Julia is seven, and regularly misunderstood because of her impulsiveness, her involvements with imaginary companions, her tendency to befriend animals from whom adults flee and her unusual prescience. With characteristic intensity, Eleanor Cameron makes vividly real Julia's inner and outer worlds.

Other titles: *Julia's Magic, A Room Made of Windows, Julia and the Hand of God* and *The Private Worlds of Julia Redfern*.

Other series: *The Wonderful Flight to the Mushroom Planet* fantasies.

☞ The Four Storey Mistake
Elizabeth Enright, illustrated by Elizabeth Enright, Heinemann, 1955 (USA). Ages 8-10 years. LIBRARY

The four storey mistake is the odd-looking house — three stories plus an afterthought in the shape of a tower — which the Melody family move to in the country. In and around it the four Melody children, Mona, Randy, Rush and Oliver, thoroughly enjoy themselves winter and summer. This book, like the others in the series of which it is a part, is an account of their adventures as they explore brook, cellar, stable,

summerhouse, hollow tree and orchard. Enright perfectly captures their excitement and the exact feel of their daily lives — in a manner which may seem slightly old-fashioned, but is absolutely authentic because the feelings of childhood are so accurately caught.
Other titles: *The Saturdays, Then There Were Five, Spiderweb for Two.*

☞ The Moffats
Eleanor Estes, illustrated by Louis Slobodkin, Harcourt Voyager, 1941 (USA). Ages 8-10 years. LIBRARY
This classic American series about a family of four children supported by their mother in a sprawling colonial house in Cranbury, New Jersey (near Princeton), hasn't lost its appeal despite its obviously dated features. Apparently mundane events — trolley rides, the sale of a house, a scary journey made by a child in a bread box, a horse and carriage ride interrupted by a storm — are recounted with a charm and humour as engaging now as they were almost a half-century ago when the series was written.
Other titles: *Rufus M, The Middle Moffat, The Moffat Museum.*

☞ Pippi Longstocking
Astrid Lindgren, illustrated by Richard Kennedy, Puffin, 1945 (Sweden). Ages 9-11 years.
LIBRARY, CHILD, GENERAL
Carrot-haired with pigtails, freckly, stronger than two grown policemen, nine years old and parentless, Pippi Longstocking lives in a cottage with a horse and a monkey and entertains herself and the neighbourhood children, Tommy and Annika. Her exploits, which include humiliating a bully, staying away from school for as long as possible and standing on a horse's back at the circus, appeal especially to venturesome girls of eight to ten. Some grown-ups may find Lindgren's manner a little frenetic.
Other titles: *Pippi Goes Aboard, Pippi in the South Seas* and many others.

☞ Ballet Shoes

Noel Streatfeild, illustrations by Ruth Gervis, Puffin, 1936 (England). Ages 10-12 years. LIBRARY

Although there are adults who will regard this series as quaint, girls of about ten or eleven continue to be fascinated by the adventures of three ballerinas, Pauline, Posy, and Petrova, the wards of an eccentric traveller named 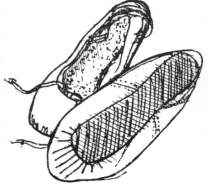 Matthew Brown ('Gum'). The three girls' efforts to become successful dancers inspire children with similar aspirations — or with altogether different ones, just because the ballerinas' exploits are so tireless and entertaining. Adults with a passion for ballet who read Streatfeild years ago claim that on this subject these dancing books have never been surpassed.

Other titles: *Dancing Shoes, White Boots* and many others.

Other series: *Thursday's Child, Far To Go.*

Books for younger readers
(8 to 12 years)

REALISM:
*Animals/
Outdoor life*

'In early summer there are plenty of things for a child to eat and drink and suck and chew. Dandelion stems are full of milk, clover heads are loaded with nectar. . . Everywhere you look is life; even the little ball of spit on the weed stalk, if you poke it apart, has a green worm inside it. And on the underside of the leaf of the potato vine are the bright orange eggs of the potato bug.'

E.B. White, *Charlotte's Web*

SINGLE NOVELS

☞ *The Broken Saddle

James Aldridge, Julia MacRae, 1982 (Australia). Ages 11-13 years. LIBRARY

This account of the complex bond between a boy and his pony is almost flawless in tone and structure. Set in the Mallee — where dust storms threaten wheat and the families responsible for growing it — the novel discloses almost as much about rural life during the Depression as about Eric's struggles to control the animal which his drover father unexpectedly gives him before he leaves home yet again. Characteristically, James Aldridge gives to every detail of his novel an authenticity missing from the works of better known writers. He deserves a much wider readership.

Other titles: *The True Story of Lilli Stubeck* (see p. 101), *The True Story of Spit MacPhee* (Guardian Award, 1987) and many others.

☞ A Dog Called George

Margaret Balderson, illustrations by Nikki Jones, Oxford, 1975 (Australia). Ages 10-12 years. LIBRARY

A blue-eyed, shaggy, devoted and apparently homeless sheepdog named George transforms the life of Tony, who is low in confidence and self-esteem until they meet.

Unsuccessful at school, and no better at making friends than at concentrating on academic subjects, Tony lives in the shadow of his

successful older siblings, and is convinced at first that people are beginning to take an interest in him solely because of George. With disarming frankness, Margaret Balderson depicts Tony's difficult struggle into greater maturity: his jealousy of everybody whose temporary affection George seeks, his unwillingness to confront the likelihood that George's real owner will reclaim him, his habitual reluctance to reach out to others and his dawning consciousness that there's a place for him in the world.

Other titles: *When Jays Fly to Barbmo* is available in some libraries.

☞ *The Midnight Fox

Betsy Byars, illustrations by Ann Grifalconi, Avon, 1968 (USA). Ages 9-11 years. LIBRARY, CHILD

Forced to spend his summer at his uncle's farm when his parents go to Europe, Tom discovers a much more exciting world than he imagined could exist. At the centre of it are a wild fox and her cub whom he carefully and secretly observes from a distance and comes to love. Byars' descriptions of these animals, and of Tom's growth, are circumspect and moving; and her use of letters written by Tom to his best friend as a means of comic relief as well as revelation is effective. The American Library Association comment on the book jacket — 'an exceptional book' — is not an exaggeration.

Other titles: *The Winged Colt of Casa Mia, Rama the Gypsy Cat* and others.

☞ *A Horse Came Running

Meindert DeJong, illustrated by Paul Sagsoorian, Macmillan, 1970 (Dutch-USA). Hans Christian Andersen Medal Winner. Ages 8-10 years. LIBRARY

After a tornado besieges his parents' farm, everything about Mark's life changes. With his father in hospital and his mother in town, his elderly neighbour Mr Sayers' wife near-fatally wounded, his ancient horse Colonel and new horse with a cut leg nowhere to be seen, he has a lot to attend to quickly.

Mark's moment by moment responses to major responsibilities are handled by DeJong with extraordinary skill and inventiveness. The novel contains many surprises, and scenes with a boy and his horse so touching that few readers will be able to forget them. DeJong's work deserves to be much more widely read in Australia than it is at present.

Other titles: *The Wheel on the School* (Newbery Medal, 1955), *Journey From Peppermint Street* (National Book Award, 1969) and many others.

☞ *Bridget and William and Horse
Jane Gardam, illustrated by Janet Rawlins, Puffin, 1984 (England). Ages 8-9 years. LIBRARY, CHILD

Two stories about children and their horses have been published together. The first, 'Bridget and William', is the more compelling; but both are good. 'Bridget and William' is about a Shetland pony given to a young girl, Bridget, as a gift by her London aunt and resisted by Bridget's father ('Horses is only for townfolks now').

The importance of William in the lives of the folk who live near Bridget is Gardam's focus; and, as usual, her narrative is just about perfect. Horse enthusiasts will treasure the entire volume.

Other titles: *The Hollow Land, The Summer After the Funeral* (see p. 107) and many others for older and younger children.

☞ Julie of the Wolves
*Jean Craighead George, illustrated by John Schoenherr,
Harper, 1972 (USA). Newbery Medal, 1973. Ages 10-12
years.* LIBRARY, CHILD

The adventures of Miyax, a young Eskimo girl who
runs away from home and is lost in the Alaskan wilds,
are engrossing though not always wholly credible.
Central to the story is Miyax's friendship with a pack of
Arctic wolves who protect and love her. Her favourite,
Amaroq, whom she eventually calls her 'adopted
father', is among the more memorable animals in the
world of children's literature. His fate becomes as
important to readers as Miyax's own.
Other titles: *My Side of the Mountain, The Talking Earth*
and others.

☞ *The Kershaw Dogs
*Helen Griffiths, illustrated by Douglas Hall, Hutchinson,
1978 (England). Ages 11-13 years.* LIBRARY

This is an extremely moving book about an
eleven-year-old boy named Dudley Kershaw, who is
brought up in Yorkshire in the 1930s by his emotionally
frozen father, Bill. Bill's sole interest is in breeding, and
getting illicit money from, fighting dogs. Thus, when
his brutal terrier Madman sires a litter, he forces
Dudley to choose a pup from it to train as a fighter.
Dudley's choice, Grip, too affectionate by nature to
want to fight, instead showers Dudley with love — the
only demonstrable feeling the boy has ever
encountered; and, of course, the animal is greatly loved
in return.

The plot turns on what Dudley is forced to do when
Grip shames him in front of all the men involved in
Kershaw dog fights by turning tail. Whether, or how,
Grip will survive this insult becomes a totally
absorbing question for all readers, whatever their age.
Other titles: *Rafa's Dog, The Wild Horse of Santander* and
many others.

☞ Papio
Victor Kelleher, Kestrel, 1984 (Australia). Ages 11-13 years. LIBRARY, CHILD, GENERAL

Saving two baboons, Papio and Upi, from the 'pointless cruelty' of African hunters who like killing for its own sake is the task of David and Jem. Their struggle to ensure the survival of animals whom they come to value enormously is dramatised by Kelleher with his accustomed flair and strong feeling. Every element of nature, in the large and impressive world of his imagining, has point and value.

Other titles: *The Hunting of Shadroth, Master of the Grove* (see p. 94) and others.

☞ Island of the Blue Dolphins
Scott O'Dell, Puffin, 1960 (USA). Newbery Medal, 1960. Hans Christian Andersen Medal Winner. Ages 10-12 years. LIBRARY, CHILD, GENERAL

This true account of a twelve-year-old Indian girl who lived alone for eighteen years on an abandoned island off the California coast when her tribe was forcibly moved from their home continues to fascinate readers, young and old. Of particular interest is Karana's relationship with the wild dog, Rontu, whom she tames and who becomes her only companion.

Other titles: *Bright Star, Bright Dawn, Streams to the River, River to the Sea* and others.

☞ *The Sign of the Beaver
Elizabeth George Speare, Gollancz, 1984 (USA). Laura Ingalls Wilder Award. Ages 11-13 years. LIBRARY

Although she has written only four novels, three of them obtainable in Australia, Speare has received a major award for the quality of her achievement. Each of the three books readily available is about a totally different world and historical period, made real in its every detail.

This one, her most recent, tells the story of Matt, a twelve-year-old boy who is temporarily in charge of the forest homestead in Maine which he has helped his father to build. While his dad brings the rest of the family from Massachusetts to their new home, Matt learns basic survival skills and much else from an Indian boy, Attean, whose grandfather has saved his life following an attack from murderous bees. Everything Matt discovers about the natural world, the knowledge of the Beaver tribe and Attean's way of life is as interesting to readers as it is to him.

Other titles: *The Bronze Bow* (see p. 64) and *The Witch of Blackbird Pond*.

☞ The Boy and the Swan
Catherine Storr, illustrated by Laszlo Acs, André Deutsch, 1987 (England). Ages 8-10 years. LIBRARY

This touching story about a boy without a name who lives in loneliness near the sea with his deaf and almost totally uncommunicative grandmother derives its power from Catherine's Storr's depiction of the lives of a family of swans whom he befriends. When the boy witnesses the deaths of a cob and his mate at a hidden pool near his Gran's cottage, he rescues the large egg which the pen has been nursing. He keeps it warm until it hatches and secretly nurtures the growing bird in his room and at the pool until his grandmother has a stroke and he is forced to go away to a children's home. How he copes and what he does to maintain contact with his cygnet will absorb adults as fully as young readers.

Other titles: *February Yowler, Puss and Cat* and others.

☞ Jodie's Journey
Colin Thiele, Rigby, 1988 (Australia). Ages 10-12 years. LIBRARY, CHILD

After twelve-year-old Jodie Carpenter wins the Greenvale Junior Show Jumping Championship on her horse Monarch, she goes steadily downhill. First she is responsible for her team's losing a race at a major school athletic event. Next she finds that her knuckles are too sore to permit her to control her horse's reins.

And eventually she discovers the reason for her increasing physical awkwardness and incapacity: rheumatoid arthritis. Because of the severity of this illness, Jodie's whole life changes. Thiele's novel details these changes, the most exciting of which occur during the Ash Wednesday bushfires of '83.

Other titles: *River Murray Mary* (see p. 66), *The Fire in the Stone* and many others. Thiele's is a conventional, though authentic, understanding of ordinary Australians.

SERIES

☞ ***Ribsy**
Beverly Cleary, illustrated by Louis Darling, Dell, 1964 (USA). Laura Ingalls Wilder Award. Ages 8-10 years.
LIBRARY, CHILD

The first of Beverly Cleary's incomparable novels about Henry Huggins' beloved black, white and brown mongrel describes Ribsy's adventures after he accidentally pushes the button that opens the window of the family car, parked at a shopping centre, and becomes lost. With her usual blend of humour and matter-of-fact good sense, Mrs Cleary presents events from Ribsy's point of view as well as from his distressed owner's in a manner so natural, endearing and timeless that few readers want the story to end, even though of course everybody is anxious for Henry's dog to be returned to the Hugginses.

Other titles in the Ribsy-Henry series: *Henry and Ribsy, Henry Huggins, Henry and the Clubhouse, Henry and the Paper Route.*

Books for younger readers
(8 to 12 years)

REALISM:
Comic adventure

'Everything matters, every time of life, and I am just as dumb and happy and silly and miserable and full of hope now as I was in the second grade. . . nothing has really changed.'

Natalie Babbitt, 'The Rhinoceros and the Pony'

'. . .inside our own older bodies are children. My son John put this unstated feeling into words once when he passed me as I looked in the mirror. "Who do you see?" he asked. "Someone younger than what your outside shows?"'

Patricia MacLachlan,
'Dialogue with Charlotte Zolotow'

SINGLE NOVELS

☞ *Harriet the Spy

Louise Fitzhugh, illustrated by Louise Fitzhugh, Dell Yearling, 1964 (USA). Ages 10-12 years. LIBRARY, CHILD

Eleven-year-old Harriet M. Welsch, who wants to be a writer, seeks excitement by 'spying' on everyone in her life and recording her observations in a notebook which she intends to be secret. What she says is extremely amusing — but not to the children in her class who discover what she thinks of them when she accidentally leaves her prize possession on the school playground. Harriet's misadventures after this minor catastrophe occurs are as diverting as those preceding it — though some of them, like the misunderstandings that occur when she is made to see a psychiatrist, may be over the heads of some readers. Fitzhugh has a perfect ear, not just for comedy, but for the characteristic foibles, strategies and ambitions of upper primary children.

Other Titles: *Nobody's Family's Going to Change, Sport* and others.

☞ Chancy and the Grand Rascal

Sid Fleischman, illustrated by Eric von Schmidt, Hamish Hamilton, 1967 (USA). Ages 9-11 years. LIBRARY

Like all of Sid Fleischman's madcap fiction, *Chancy and the Grand Rascal* is a tall tale. An orphan whose father died in the Civil War, Chancy B. Dundee leaves his farmer-master to roam the Midwest and search for his younger brothers and sisters. Along the Ohio River he encounters a colonel named Plugg who tricks him into parting with a gold coin for eggs with triple yolks, a wide-shouldered man in a slouch hat who turns out to be his uncle Will Buckthorn, the Grand Rascal, and a host of other colourful characters — many of them rogues — with names like Hawk Pewitt and Micajah Jones. With Will's help, what's lost is found in ways that parody America's wackier Westerns.

Other titles: *The Whipping Boy* (Newbery Medal, 1987), *The Ghost in the Noonday Sun* and many others.

☞ *The Turbulent Term of Tyke Tyler
Gene Kemp, illustrated by Carolyn Dinan, Puffin, 1977 (England). Carnegie Medal, 1977. Ages 10-12 years.
LIBRARY, CHILD, GENERAL

This account of the trouble Tyke Tyler gets into, aided and abetted by young, slow Danny Price, ends with a witty twist which many readers don't anticipate. What everyone cannot help responding to is the vitality of Gene Kemp's comic portrait of Cricklepit Combined School and its 4M class. Whether Tyke is trying to protect Danny's stolen ten pound note, slipping in slime while trying to get him bones he wants, fighting with Big Boots Kneeshaw, helping Danny (over and over) to prepare for a major test, or trying to save him from the charge of stealing a watch, the novel has absolute authenticity and charm. All of Gene Kemp's books do.

Other titles: *The Well, Gowie Corby Plays Chicken, Tamworth Pig and the Litter* (see p. 88) and many others.

☞ From the Mixed-Up Files of Mrs Basil E. Frankweiler
E.L. Konigsburg, illustrated by E.L. Konigsburg, Macmillan, 1967 (USA). Newbery Medal, 1968. Ages 10-12 years. LIBRARY, CHILD

The story of Claudia and Jamie's protracted visit to the Metropolitan Museum of Art in New York City is as ingenious as the book's title and certainly as unusual. The two children get to the museum — and sleep in a four-poster bed, bathe in the water surrounding a fountain display, eat with groups of visiting school children, scrutinise exhibits and become deeply attached to a statue of an angel which may or may not have been the work of Michelangelo — because they've run away from home. Returning to their parents once they've reached the end of their money and resources isn't any easier than walking blocks and blocks in the vicinity of the museum trying to save their dwindling hoard. But the way that it happens is as amusing and surprising as their time away.

Other titles: *Jennifer, Hecate, Macbeth and Me* and *George*.

☞ Staying Alive in Year 5

John Marsden, Pan Books, 1989 (Australia). Ages 9-11 years. LIBRARY, CHILD, GENERAL

The rules for Mr Murlin's Year 5 pupils are announced within the first few minutes of their arrival: 'There's to be no cooking Lamingtons in the classroom. Students must keep breathing at all times while in here. You are not to ride skateboards across the desks. I keep a chainsaw in the cupboard for people who wear glasses without a licence. Crocodiles are to be put in the box marked "Crocodiles", not in your desks. . .' What follows is perfectly in keeping with this startling announcement: a sequence of events uncommon in Australian classrooms or in classrooms anywhere, even in King Arthur's day.

Other titles: *So Much to Tell You. . .* (see p. 114).

☞ My Simple Little Brother

Lilith Norman, illustrated by David Rae, Collins, 1979 (Australia). Ages 8-10 years. LIBRARY

Literal-minded Fieldsy creates endless difficulties for his family in this wacky chronicle of the bizarre effects of linguistic bewilderment. Raining buckets, butter fingers, father losing his head, a visitor eating like a horse and other common figures of speech become in

Fieldsy's world occasions for fundamental misunderstanding. Even educational jargon — 'the potential of television in an unstructured learning situation is unlimited' — assumes for him (at this point in time) an importance that is disproportionate. Both reluctant readers and more seasoned students of comedy will be charmed by Lilith Norman's excursion into absurdity.

Other titles: *Climb a Lonely Hill, Mocking Bird Man* and others.

☞ *The Great Gilly Hopkins

Katherine Paterson, Avon, 1978 (USA). National Book Award, 1979. Ages 11-13 years.
LIBRARY, CHILD, GENERAL

This is probably the best loved, and certainly the funniest, of the author's greatly admired novels. Its protagonist, Galadriel Hopkins, the eleven-year-old illegitimate daughter of a flower child, shunted from one temporary home to the next, is as witty and astute as she is obstreperous. It takes a rare person — fat, uneducated Mamie Trotter, foster mother of a series of impossible children, and the most lovable of all of Katherine Paterson's characters — to tame her.

But Trotter doesn't accomplish this tough task alone. She is helped in her battle to cleanse Gilly's battered heart by her blind coloured neighbour, Mr Randall, her other foster child, unnaturally timid William Ernest, and Gilly's spirited black teacher, Miss Harris. Together, this unlikely group of Christians helps Gilly to acquire a sense of herself and of her place.

Other titles: *The Master Puppeteer* (National Book Award, 1977), *Bridge to Terabithia* (see p. 115) and many others.

SERIES

☞ The Not-Just-Anybody Family
Betsy Byars, Piper-Bodley Head, 1986 (USA). Ages 10-12 years. LIBRARY, CHILD, GENERAL

This series about the poor but happy Blossom family — Vern, Maggie, Junior, their mother Vicki, their grandfather Pap and Mud the dog — who recover from one scrape after another with spunky good will, has immense charm. In this novel, the first of four set in the rural South, a fall from a barn roof, the secret invasion of a jail cell and the disappearance of a yellow mongrel highlight adventures characterised by real danger but an unmistakable spirit of hopefulness.

Other titles in the series: *The Blossoms Meet the Vulture Lady, The Blossoms and the Green Phantom, A Blossom Promise.*

☞ *Ramona the Pest
Beverly Cleary, illustrated by Louis Darling, Scholastic, 1968 (USA). Ages 8-10 years.
LIBRARY, CHILD, GENERAL

Ramona Quimby must be one of the most fetching little

girls in children's literature. In this, the first book of Beverly Cleary's delightful series, she starts school, gets into all kinds of trouble, goes into ecstasies and depressions over her beloved teacher Miss Binney, misunderstands key things said to her ('Sit here for the present' — i.e. 'Sit here until I give you a gift') and in general amuses and maddens everyone in her vicinity. Remarkably, her adventures have not dated in the slightest over a thirty year period and readers of all ages — but especially those starting out — continue to be entertained by her well-intentioned blunders.

Other titles in the series: *Ramona the Brave, Beezus and Ramona, Ramona and Her Father, Ramona and Her Mother* and others.

Other series: The *Henry Huggins* books and the *Ribsy* books (see p. 39).

☞ Penny Pollard's Letters
Robin Klein, illustrated by Ann James, Oxford, 1984 (Australia). Ages 10-12 years.
LIBRARY, CHILD, GENERAL

This collection of letters, purported to be written by a ten-year-old, is very popular with upper primary children. Penny's obsession with horses, her photos of everything she writes about including a molar removed by one Mrs Lansell at the age of thirteen, her spontaneous criticisms of silly or unfair people (Alistair's mother 'never looks at any of the great inventions he's made in the toolshed, she just says, "Alistair, tidy up all that mess you left lying around"') and her undiluted enthusiasms or dislikes ('I don't like any of the names on the list you sent me, especially not *Jason*') entertain boys as well as girls — though, mostly, girls.

Other titles in the series: *Penny Pollard's Diary, Penny Pollard's Guide to Modern Manners.*

☞ Anastasia Krupnik
Lois Lowry, Lions, 1979 (USA). Ages 9-11 years.
LIBRARY, CHILD, GENERAL

Ten-year-old Anastasia Krupnik has a green notebook

in which she keeps private information — possible beginnings of poems, lists of her favourite words and her pet loves and hates, and important events and facts. Her life is amusing, slightly chaotic and often unmanageable, even though she is very bright and the child of very bright parents (an English professor and an artist).

Lowry's charming book and its successors involve readers in Anastasia's preoccupations even when they're very different from their own. Her lists (which take up full pages) and her madcap struggles with friends and family are especially appealing.

Other titles: *Anastasia Again!, Anastasia At Your Service* and many others.

Books for younger readers (8 to 12 years)

REALISM:
Mysterious adventure

'All children like adventure, and not just for the excitement of what happens next. . . In adventure stories [children] can see themselves taking part in the action and not only that. They can also test themselves, measure themselves against the characters in the book. Would they be brave . . . or would they run away? Would they be honest, or would they lie?'

Nina Bawden, 'A Dead Pig and My Father'

SINGLE NOVELS

☞ **The Trial of Anna Cotman**
Vivien Alcock, Methuen, 1989 (England). Ages 10-12 years. LIBRARY

Vivien Alcock is extremely good at creating suspense and in rendering the inexplicable. But her interest in the sinister, apparent in some of her novels and not others, is unsettling. Here, it is expressed in a persuasive account of the pressures exerted upon a girl new to a school and neighbourhood. When Anna Cotman, an orphan, moves to a flat above a wool shop with her devoted grandmother, she is immediately taken up by a friendless girl named Lindy Miller and ushered into a secret club whose members wear masks and issue orders.

Very quickly the orders become insupportable; and the plot hinges on what Anna will do about them. Because bullying is such a problem for the young, and also because Alcock handles one of its most extreme and distasteful forms so realistically, the novel has a place in a wide reading program.

Other titles: *The Mysterious Mr Ross, The Sylvia Game* and others.

☞ **Little Brother**
Allan Baillie, illustrated by Elizabeth Honey, Nelson, 1985 (Australia). Ages 11-13 years.
LIBRARY, CHILD, GENERAL

This account of the effect of the 1970s conflict in South-East Asia on the lives of two orphaned brothers creates a suspense which is sustained until the very last sentence. Vithy's search for Mang, when the two are separated, takes him through jungles, mountains and perils so graphically rendered that the Cambodia created by Pol Pot becomes wholly real for readers too young to have witnessed scenes of torture on TV or viewed *The Killing Fields* when it first came out.

Other titles: Baillie's other books for upper primary

children, such as *Adrift* and *Eagle Island*, despite being full of adventure, do not work as well as this one.

☞ The Curse of the Egyptian Mummy

Pat Hutchins, illustrated by Laurence Hutchins, Lions, 1983 (England). Ages 8-9 years. LIBRARY, CHILD

Pat Hutchins specialises in outlandish comic mysteries, and this one hinges on the discovery of an Egyptian treasure. The unlikely setting for escapades worthy of the late Peter Sellers is a beautiful camping ground used annually by groups like the 15th Hampstead Cub Scouts. Such bizarre occurrences as the appearance in the area of an asp, the ransacking of the Cub Scouts' camp, and the aggressive dunking of a child by an unknown adult in Wellington boots will intrigue most young readers. Laurence Hutchins' amusing drawings are a perfect accompaniment to the text.

Other titles: *Follow That Bus!*, *The Mona Lisa Mystery* and others.

☞ Challenge in the Dark

Robert Leeson, illustrated by Jim Russell, Collins, 1978 (England). Ages 8-9 years. LIBRARY, CHILD

Although Leeson's prose is undistinguished and his plotting a bit creaky, he knows how children think and plan, especially in response to dangers it would be best for adults not to know about. With the help of his friends Ranji, Sandra, and Andrew — all the children in *The Demon Bike Rider* — Michael Baxter works to extricate himself from bully Sam Taylor. Against his better judgment, he agrees to spend time with Sam's younger brother Steven in a terrifyingly dark and perilous underground shelter built for wartime, but still accessible to intrepid youngsters. The grim excitement of this venture will appeal to younger readers, particularly boys.

Other titles: *The Demon Bike Rider*, *Grange Hill Goes Wild* and others.

☞ The Road to Sattin Shore

Philippa Pearce, illustrated by Charlotte Voake, Puffin,
1983 (England). Ages 10-12 years.
LIBRARY, CHILD, GENERAL

Mystery assumes an even more central place in this absorbing novel than it does in others of Pearce's acclaimed books for younger and older children. Kate Tranter's secret efforts to find out all she can about her missing (presumed dead) father, his drowned brother and all the people who know anything about them take her far from home on lonely, fatiguing bicycle rides. They also issue in eerie and surprising happenings in the upper storeys of her house. Finally, with the help of her older brothers, she begins to unravel crucial facts about family events which took place ten years before. The unravelling process is intensely interesting.

Other titles: *Tom's Midnight Garden* (see p. 75), *The Minnow on the Say* and others.

☞ To the Wild Sky

Ivan Southall, illustrated by Jennifer Tuckwell, Puffin,
1968 (Australia). Australian Book of the Year, 1968.
Ages 10-12 years. LIBRARY, CHILD

To the Wild Sky depicts four boys and two girls who survive a plane crash and are forced to cope alone with all of the ensuing difficulties. Upper primary readers who like open-ended adventures consider this novel, and others by Southall about children fighting natural disasters without adult help, engrossing. But many children (and adults like me) find his characterisation flat, his plots predictable and his prose dull. He has won the Australian Children's Book of the Year Award three times.

Other titles: *Ash Road, Hills End* and many others.

☞ *Tom Tiddler's Ground

John Rowe Townsend, illustrated by Mark Peppé, Viking Kestrel, 1985 (England). Ages 10-12 years.

LIBRARY, CHILD

When Vic and his companions Brian ("Brain"), Sam, Mary-Lou and Darryl find a waste patch with a half-wrecked cabin on their local canal, they begin spending a lot of time exploring its possibilities. Their discovery of hidden pennies and a horse-brass which Mary-Lou insists is gold involves them in far more than they anticipate. With his usual care and narrative flair, Townsend resolves the mystery surrounding 'Tom Tiddler's Ground' and provides interesting snippets of history about the canal on which the children row their makeshift boat. Very few writers are as good as he is at creating, all at once, mystery and danger, a historic sense of place and a lively group of characters to solve knotty problems.

Other titles: *Top of the World, Gumble's Yard* and many others (for older children as well — e.g. *The Intruder,* Globe/Horn Book Award, 1970).

Books for younger readers
(8 to 12 years)

REALISM:
Historical adventure

'Things familiar become invisible, and it is only when we move them to another place or another time that their qualities leap out at us. A favourite picture, reframed, becomes almost a new picture, and we remember what it was that first attracted us.'

Leon Garfield,
'Historical Fiction for Our Global Times'

SINGLE NOVELS

☞ Sounder
William Armstrong, illustrated by Jim Russell, Puffin,
1969, (USA). Newbery Medal, 1970. Ages 10-12 years.
LIBRARY

A powerful movie was made from this slim, relatively
undemanding book about a Southern Negro family
whose father is wrongly imprisoned in the early years
of this century. The novel takes its title from a dog, half
bulldog and half hound, whose devotion to everyone in
the family helps to keep them going during a period of
intense adversity. Even when he is badly wounded by
brutal white men, Sounder refuses to be beaten. The
family is like that too — which helps to explain why so
many Australian schools use the book as a text for
reluctant and average readers. Armstrong's language
is simple, and his sympathy for the underdog is strong.

☞ Mouldy's Orphan
Gillian Avery, illustrated by Faith Jacques, Collins, 1978
(England). Ages 8-10 years. LIBRARY

Like most of Gillian Avery's slightly quaint and comic
fiction, this short novel for beginning readers is set in
late Victorian England. Molly Kippins — called
Mouldy because that's how her hair looks to other
children — is obsessed with orphans. After reading a
novel on the subject called *Froggy's Little Brother*, she
decides she'd like an orphan for herself, to protect and
care for. On a school excursion to a pantomime at
Oxford she finds one (Benjy), brings him home and
insists on keeping him despite strong parental
opposition. The fate of Benjy and Mouldy together is
the subject of the rest of the book. Faith Jacques'
drawings are, as usual, perfect.
Other titles: *The Greatest Gresham, A Likely Lad*
(Guardian Award, 1972) and others.

☞ Carrie's War

*Nina Bawden, illustrated by Faith Jacques, Puffin, 1973
(England). Ages 10-13 years.*
LIBRARY, CHILD, GENERAL

When London is bombed during World War II,
twelve-year-old Carrie and her ten-year-old brother
Nick are evacuated to Wales. There they are billeted
with a put-upon single woman, 'Aunt Lou' Evans, and
her mean-spirited brother, a Councillor. Only at their
friend Albert's home, Druid's Bottom, which is run by
a generous working woman named Hepzibah Green,
do they enjoy themselves. But what happens to them
at both places is important and instructive. The sources
of deep feuds in the Evans family come to light, as do
key facts about all of the inhabitants of Druid's Bottom.
Other titles: *Squib, The Peppermint Pig* and many others.

☞ Longtime Passing

*Hesba Brinsmead, Puffin, 1971 (Australia). Australian
Children's Book of the Year, 1972. Ages 11-13 years.*
LIBRARY, CHILD, GENERAL

In Candlebark Country in the Blue Mountains, the
Truelance family build Longtime. After it is finally
completed, the five Truelance children and their
parents come to know every bit of clear area and bush
near their property. Brinsmead chronicles the period
— early this century — and the place with a devotion
which gives her book a unique verisimilitude.
Ordinary events — shepherding bullocks, buying new
clothes, exploring a bush trail, attending the races,
filling the billy — are portrayed with a detailed
attentiveness which intermediate readers can
appreciate.
Other titles: *Pastures of the Blue Crane, Once There Was a
Swagman* and others.

☞ Dust of the Earth
Vera and Bill Cleaver, Oxford, 1975 (USA). Ages 11-13 years. LIBRARY

Although the events described in this vivid account of life in the South Dakota badlands aren't given a date, the family whose daily existence we share calls itself pioneering. Through the eyes of fourteen-year-old Fern Drawn, we learn exactly what it was like to raise sheep almost by accident in isolated country, with nothing to count on except adversity.

When the Drawns inherit a farm from their grandfather, a snobbish man who would have regarded them as 'the dust of the earth', they move to Chokecherry. There they experience foul winds and heat, blizzards so fierce that they destroy anything in their path, rejection by townspeople and daily threats to their livelihood — the worst of them being a gray wolf who almost kills their dog and destroys three of their sheep. The result of this hardship is that they come to value one another in a new way.

Other titles: *Where the Lilies Bloom, Trial Valley* and other respected novels mainly for older children.

☞ *Dawn of Fear
Susan Cooper, illustrated by Margery Gill, Puffin, 1970 (England). Ages 10-13 years. LIBRARY, CHILD

'Derek saw, then, one thing that he recognised and that told him this unimaginable chaotic ruin had indeed once been the Hutchinses' house. He saw that the front gate was still there.' This description of the  results of a London bombing during World War II comes near the end of Susan Cooper's splendid, partly autobiographical novel.

Like everything else in the understated last section of the book, its power depends on the accumulated effects of the everyday events of the previous chapters: the building of a camp by Derek, his best friend Peter and their other close friends; the bombing raids which regularly interrupt life, day or night; the ongoing battles of two rival groups of boys; the burial of animals killed by German bombs; and the scrutiny of objects which may or may not be dangerous.

Everything about the book — its dialogue, its story line, its descriptions of people and places in London — is beautifully managed. I don't know a more authentic war story for readers 10 to 13.

Other titles: *The Dark Is Rising* series (see p. 156) and others.

☞ The Green Wind

Thurley Fowler, Rigby, 1985 (Australia). Australian Children's Book of the Year, 1986. Ages 10-13 years.
LIBRARY, CHILD, GENERAL

Family and school squabbles, the effort to make friends, the constraints affecting fruit-growing families like her own, the sights and smells of rural life, what to include in Show Day entries, how to cure sick animals or dented bicycles and what to concentrate on for the future preoccupy eleven-year-old Jennifer Robinson in this account of life in New South Wales in the late 1940s. Fowler's treatment of these and related matters is always down-to-earth, accurate and unaffected. She appeals to a wide range of readers.

Other titles: *Wait for Me! Wait for Me!, The Youngest One* and others.

☞ *Smith

Leon Garfield, illustrated by Antony Maitland, Puffin, 1967 (England). Ages 10-12 years. LIBRARY, CHILD

Twelve-year-old Smith, a pickpocket roaming around the slums of St Paul's in eighteenth century London, is temporarily rescued from the clutches of two seasoned adult criminals by a blind judge named Mr Mansfield. Living in his Vine Street house utterly changes Smith's life, not least because Mr Mansfield's daughter is as kind to him as her father is. Together, the Mansfields make a decent boy of him — initially, by giving him a bath that takes almost three hours. In the end, he beats the criminals at their own game through a complex process full of excitement and surprises.

Garfield's language is witty and demanding; his characterisation is robust; and his story has wide appeal. Readers who respond enthusiastically to this novel will almost certainly like others of his books set in England in the 1700s.

Other titles: *Black Jack, The Apprentices* and many others. Worth noting is that, with Edmund Blishen, Garfield has written two fine and difficult-to-acquire collections of Greek myth (for older children), each held together by a single narrative line: *The God Beneath the Sea* and *The Golden Shadow*.

☞ Ask Me No Questions

Ann Schlee, Macmillan, 1976 (England). Ages 11-13 years. LIBRARY

Because of a cholera epidemic in London, Laura and her younger brother Barty are sent by their clergyman father to live with a forbidding aunt and her family. Next door is an orphanage which nobody living in the town, including all of the professed Christians in Aunt Bolinger's circle, wants to know or talk about. Through her encounters with some of the disgracefully neglected children who live there and who are prepared to eat pig's slop in preference to the food they are normally given, Laura discovers what it is to be her brother's keeper. On the power of ignorant social pressure, and the difficulties imposed on a lonely child by her own moral courage, Mrs Schlee is very good indeed.

Other titles: *The Consul's Daughter, The Vandal* (Guardian Award, 1979) and others.

☞ The Singing Tree
Kate Seredy, illustrated by Imre Hofbauer Knight, 1940 (Hungary). Ages 10-12 years. LIBRARY, CHILD

The ordinary activities of rural life — caring for animals and the land, celebrating a wedding, going to a country dance — are entirely disrupted by World War I, which takes all of the able men in Kate Seredy's story to the trenches. To what extent a somewhat sentimental translation has marred what is by now a children's classic isn't clear; but even some embarrassingly purple passages don't spoil an instructive social and family history. Attitudes peculiar to Eastern Europe during the earlier part of this century — towards Hungarian Jews, war veterans, homeless waifs trapped by international conflict and suffering mothers and children — give this sequel to *The Good Master* a cutting edge.

Other titles: *The Good Master, The White Stag.*

☞ *The Bronze Bow
Elizabeth George Speare, Puffin, 1961 (USA). Newbery Medal, 1961. Laura Ingalls Wilder Award. Ages 10-13 years. LIBRARY, CHILD

Daniel's hatred of the Roman conquerors who crucified his father is fuelled by the young Jewish guerillas whose band, led by a cynical man called Rosh, he joins in the Galilean hills. Ultimately, his attitudes towards the Romans are radically altered by a teacher called Jesus, whom he hears several times and comes to value in spite of himself, and by his good friends Joel and Thracia, who are also profoundly influenced by this same teacher. The process of change in Daniel is unpredictable and always

interesting — not least because of the rich background of history surrounding it. The *Guardian* exaggerates only a little in calling the story more worthy than 'a thousand sermons'.

Other titles: *The Witch of Blackbird Pond* and *The Sign of the Beaver* (see p. 37).

☞ Me and Jeshua
Eleanor Spence, illustrated by Shane Conroy, Dove, 1984 (Australia). Ages 10-12 years. LIBRARY, CHILD

In this beautifully appointed book, Eleanor Spence imagines what it might have been like to be Jude, cousin of Jeshua, living in Israel 2000 years ago. Tracing their lineage, beginning with their grandfather Yakim, Spence describes the daily lives of apparently ordinary people who are far from ordinary. Jeshua's father, Josef, husband of Miriam, is not really his father. And Jeshua himself has a love for others, and a belief in a personal God to whom one can speak, which set him apart. Eleanor Spence's strong evocation of place — the Great Lake, the City of the Holy Mountain, the Town of Branches — complements her

lively portraiture. Young readers unfamiliar with the essential Christian story are likely to want to know more after encountering this introduction to it.

Other titles: *Lillypilly Hill, A Candle for St Antony* (see p. 118) and others.

☞ *Warrior Scarlet
*Rosemary Sutcliff, illustrated by Charles Keeping,
Oxford, 1958 (England). Ages 10-13 years.*
LIBRARY, CHILD, GENERAL

During the Bronze Age, young men training to be warriors had to spend three years in the Boys' House before undergoing an arduous rite of passage into manhood. The most difficult test facing Sutcliff's young hero, Drem, during this crucial period involves the killing of a wolf unaided. Failure means exile from his tribe and consignment to the ranks of the Dark People — shepherds, not warriors. But success appears an almost unrealisable dream, because he is crippled in one arm.

Among the fascinating issues inseparable from this central one, and explored in full in the novel, are the place of hunting in Drem's world, the situation of women, the nature of heroism and honour and the role of adults in guiding the young. Like others of Rosemary Sutcliff's classic tales, it has an impressively strong narrative line, but its tone is sometimes a bit feverish.

Other titles: *The Eagle of the Ninth, The Lantern Bearers* (Carnegie Medal, 1959) and many other acclaimed books about England's early history.

☞ River Murray Mary
*Colin Thiele, illustrated by Robert Ingpen (in hard cover),
Rigby, 1979 (Australia). Ages 10-12 years.*
LIBRARY, CHILD, GENERAL

This lively tale about the adventures of Mary Agnes Baker, who lives with her family at Gum Flat Farm on the banks of the Murray during the depression of the 1920s, describes such events as the encounter of Mary and her dog Snap with a tiger snake, the building of a weir along the river and the arrival of terrible floods which threaten not only the Baker family but the entire region. Like all of Colin Thiele's novels, this one will appeal to readers with a strong interest in the Australian countryside and its past.

Other titles: *Jodie's Journey* (see p. 38), *The Valley Between* (Australian Children's Book of the Year, 1982) and many others.

☞ Seven Little Australians
Ethel Turner, Ward, Lock, 1894 (Australia). Ages 10-12 years. LIBRARY, CHILD, GENERAL

Although this classic has quaint features, much of its language — 'You are a horrid old pig. . . an' I hates you hard. . . an' I wis' a drate big ziant would come and huff and puff and blow you into ze middlest part of ze sea' — is surprisingly modern, as are the scrapes the naughtier Woolcots get into. Readers will strongly sympathise with Judy, forced to leave her brothers and sisters for boarding school, or Meg, suffering a fainting fit after enduring a series of domestic stresses; but few will be able to predict a death in the family in the last section of the book. Amid adventures and festivities, this death comes as a shock; but it's as central to Turner's portrait of Australian life in the 1890s as the noisier exploits of the Woolcot younger children.

☞ The Miller's Boy
Barbara Willard, illustrated by Gareth Floyd, Penguin, 1976 (England). Ages 11-13 years. LIBRARY, CHILD

Twelve-year-old Thomas Welfare, orphaned, lives with his near-mad grandfather, Gaffer, at Gospels Mill in Sussex, works as hard as a man, and wonders about his future. The year is 1478. When a boy named Lewis Mallory, whose lineage is superior to Thomas's, enters the world of the mill, young Welfare's prospects change, though not in any obvious way. Only at the book's end does it become clear that vivid events in the boys' daily round — the making of a blood pact, a storm that hurls a man to his death, a moonlit horse ride — have made it possible for Thomas to live a much freer life than Gaffer was able to do. Barbara Willard's portrait of the age, the place and every individual life touching Thomas's is fascinating and moving.

Other titles: *Field and Forest, The Iron Lily* (see p. 139).

SERIES

☞ Tom Fobble's Day

Alan Garner, etchings by Michael Foreman, Collins, 1977 (England). Ages 8-9 years. LIBRARY

Alan Garner's unusual quartet, which can be read aloud, recreates the world inhabited by a Victorian stonecutter and his descendants near a place called Wood Hill. Evocative language, peculiar to the time and place rendered, distinguishes each book and can be understood despite its strangeness ('I feel the wind's bristled up. . . I'll not come out'). *Tom Fobble's Day*, the second in the series, tells the story of William, whose sledge is 'Tom Fobbled' by an intimidating boy named Stewart Allman, who makes up his own rules about who owns what. When William's grandfather, a smith, builds William another sledge, he handles it with an agility no other child can manage.

Other titles in the series: *The Stone Book, Granny Reardun, The Aimer Gate.*

☞ Viking's Dawn

Henry Treece, illustrated by Christine Price, Puffin, 1955 (England). Ages 10-12 years. LIBRARY, CHILD

A Norse proverb cited by Harald Sigurdson, the young protagonist of *Viking's Dawn*, goes: 'Praise no day till evening, no sword until tested, no ice until crossed, and no ale until it has been drunk.' As well as knowing the value of caution, Harald and his older voyaging companions understand the importance of extreme physical and mental toughness. Their lives aboard the vessel 'Nameless' in the year 780 AD are constantly at the mercy of storms, attacks from other vessels, piracy, illness or other bodily incapacity, and treachery from within their own ranks. Although Treece's dialogue is stilted and his diction somewhat purple from time to time, his vision of the Vikings' nature, and their whole manner of existence, has the ring of truth.

Other titles in the series: *The Road to Miklagard, Viking's Sunset.*

☞ *Little House on the Prairie

Laura Ingalls Wilder, illustrated by Garth Williams,
Puffin, 1935 (USA). Ages 8-10 years.
LIBRARY, CHILD, GENERAL

The 'Little House' books, considered classics, are unfamiliar to many people despite the TV series (which bears little resemblance to them). Like all her early books about the arduous existence of pioneers like the Ingalls family, this one contains fascinating snippets of social history as well as vivid portraits of daily life in a covered wagon and then a log cabin somewhere between Wisconsin and the far West. How this cabin is built, the survival skills necessary for even very young children to master, the importance of necessities we all take for granted, the unimaginable joy of Christmas and the horror of a prairie fire are only some of the large subjects memorably covered.

Other titles in the series: *Little House in the Big Woods, On the Banks of Plum Creek, The Long Winter, By the Shores of Silver Lake* and others.

Books for younger readers (8 to 12 years)

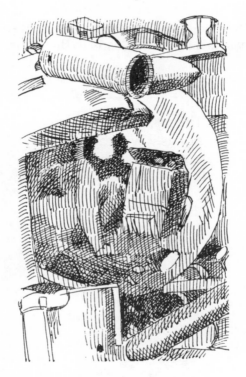

FANTASY:
Time travel

'All times co-exist and the future can sometimes affect the past, even though the past is a road that leads to the future.'

Susan Cooper, *Silver on the Tree*

'Time as it is cannot stay,
nor as it was cannot be.
Dissolving and passing away
are the world, the ages and me.'

Jill Paton Walsh, *A Chance Child*

SINGLE NOVELS

☞ ***Tuck Everlasting**
   Natalie Babbitt, Lions, 1975 (England). Ages 10-12 years.
   LIBRARY, CHILD

Instead of running away from home as she would like to do, Winnie Foster is kidnapped by a remarkable family, the Tucks, who are doomed always to remain as they were when they accidentally drank water from a magic spring. Because it is her job to safeguard this family secret, Winnie finds herself in apparently endless strife. A stranger in a yellow suit follows her in order to cash in on the spring; Mae Tuck is put in jail and is in desperate need of Winnie as rescuer; and Jesse Tuck, from whom Winnie is forced to part, presses her to rejoin him at the age of seventeen and live with the Tucks forever. From page one, Natalie Babbitt blends humour and pathos, suspense and philosophic deftness as comfortably as anyone writing in English today.
Other titles: *The Search for Delicious, Goody Hall* and others.

☞ **Tangara**
   Nan Chauncy, illustrated by Brian Wildsmith, Oxford, 1960 (Australia). Australian Children's Book of the Year Award, 1961. Ages 10-12 years.
   LIBRARY, CHILD

An old necklace given to Lexie Pavemont when she returns from boarding school to her home in rural Tasmania initiates a series of adventures which take her back in time to the world inhabited by an Aboriginal girl, Merrina, and her tribe. As well as providing essential information about Merrina's people, and contrasting it with biased 'facts' Lexie is given in history lessons at school, the novel dramatises the difficulties and pleasures attending a person's introduction to an entirely new and strange culture. It demands a lot from upper primary readers but, like other books by Chauncy on Aboriginal life, it rewards attentiveness.

Other titles: *Tiger in the Bush, Mathinna's People* (for older readers) and others.

☞ Charlotte Sometimes

Penelope Farmer, illustrated by Chris Connor, Chatto and Windus, 1969 (England). Ages 10-13 years. LIBRARY

Set in a British boarding school in the late 1950s, this well-loved story about time and selfhood takes its introverted heroine, thirteen-year-old Charlotte Makepeace, back to 1918 and World War I. For reasons which don't become clear for some time, on the morning after her first night at *Cedar*, Charlotte finds that she has become a different thirteen-year-old: Clare Moby, who slept in the very same bed and room forty years earlier. Soon afterwards she realises that she can move back and forwards in time, changing places with Clare and living her life — being Charlotte only sometimes.

As well as creating large identity problems, this situation exposes Charlotte to a host of fatiguing difficulties connected with wartime. Despite the melancholy, sometimes grotesque, timbre of her existence, however, the novel isn't depressing; it is at times encouraging and instructive.

Other titles: *Saturday by Seven, The Summer Birds* and others hard to obtain.

☞ The Wild Hunt of Hagworthy

Penelope Lively, illustrated by Juliet Mozley, Heinemann, 1971 (England). Ages 10-13 years. LIBRARY

In the village of Hagworthy in Somerset, a medieval dance has been revived to raise money for a church fête. A young girl, Lucy, who is visiting her aunt there after a gap of five years, is troubled by the Horn Dance and by much else going on in the area — especially, conventional pressures exerted upon the young, and in particular upon a friend from childhood, the blacksmith's nephew Kester. Unlike some of Lively's other books for intelligent children, which blend history, realism, and fantasy in ways that are witty but curiously inert, this one fairly races. In this respect, it resembles her more successful books for adults.

Other titles: *The Ghost of Thomas Kempe* (Carnegie Medal, 1973), *The House in Norham Gardens* (for older readers) and others.

☞ Tom's Midnight Garden

Philippa Pearce, illustrated by Susan Einzig, Oxford, 1958 (England). Ages 10-12 years.
LIBRARY, CHILD, GENERAL

By now almost a classic in the genre, *Tom's Midnight Garden* creates a magical world, unbound by time as it is usually conceived, in a garden made real by a clock's striking thirteen. Bundled off to a boring aunt and uncle when his brother gets the measles, Tom has nothing to occupy him until he discovers the wonders released by the grandfather clock in the hall of their flat. Chief among his momentous finds is Hattie, a girl living during a much earlier period than his own, much abused by members of her family, and an increasingly dear companion to him despite the enormous differences in their circumstances.

Their many meetings, unpredictable in nature and difficult for Tom to connect in a coherent pattern, are as memorable to us as they are to him. Particularly vivid is an ice-skating scene in the latter half of the book.

Other titles: *The Road to Sattin Shore* (see p. 55), *Minnow on the Say* and others.

☞ The Best-Kept Secret

Emily Rodda, illustrated by Noela Young, Angus and Robertson, 1988 (Australia). Australian Junior Book of the Year Award, 1989. Ages 8-9 years. LIBRARY, CHILD

Like Emily Rodda's better-known *Pigs Might Fly*, this novel is both popular and highly regarded. A species of fantasy quite different from its predecessor, *The Best-Kept Secret* is about a magic carousel which allows its riders to travel forward into time as much as seven years. When young Jo discovers this carousel on her own Marley Street, arriving overnight from nowhere, she can't decide whether to ride on it.

Eventually she takes the risk and, as a result, makes a series of fascinating discoveries about the forms the future is going to take in her own neighbourhood and nearby. In a very short space, Emily Rodda creates an engrossing picture of Jo's experiences in different time realms.

Other titles: *Pigs Might Fly* (Australian Junior Book of the Year 1987), *Something Special*.

SERIES

☞ *The Children of Green Knowe

Lucy Boston, illustrated by Peter Boston, Puffin, 1954 (England). Ages 10-12 years. LIBRARY, CHILD

When a small boy named Tolly comes to stay with his great-grandmother Mrs Oldknow in her ancestral house by a river at Green Knowe — pronounced Noah, and very dear to Lucy Boston herself — she delights him with stories about three children who grew up there in the 1600s and died in the Great Plague. The little girl, Linnet, the boy Toby and his pony Feste, and their brother Alexander become so real to Tolly that he enters their lives, as they do his. Lucy Boston's magical evocation of a place, and her assumption that imaginative people can travel in time, have influenced countless other writers of fantasy. They have also produced several generations of readers devoted to

Green Knowe.
Other titles in the series: *Treasure at Green Knowe, The River at Green Knowe, A Stranger at Green Knowe, An Enemy at Green Knowe.*

☞ *The Lion, the Witch and the Wardrobe

*C.S. Lewis illustrated by Pauline Baynes, Lions, 1950 (England). Ages 8-12 years.*LIBRARY, CHILD, GENERAL

Although Lewis's Narnia chronicles are extremely well known, there are children and parents starting out who are not familiar with them. Many people's favourite, *The Lion, the Witch and the Wardrobe* introduces young Lucy, Edmund, Peter and Susan to another world altogether, as they move through the door of a mysterious wardrobe in a room in a professor's huge house into a snowy landscape presided over by a wicked witch whose special form of bribery is Turkish Delight. Their adventures, which involve them in spiritual battles suitable for persons their age, do not end when an unusual death and rebirth takes place near the end of the book, but continue in six other novels beautifully suited to being read aloud.

Other titles in the series: *The Magician's Nephew, The Horse and His Boy, Prince Caspian, The Voyage of the Dawn Treader, The Silver Chair, The Last Battle.*

Books for younger readers (8 to 12 years)

FANTASY:
Talking creatures

'I am almost inclined to set it up as a canon that a children's story which is enjoyed only by children is a bad children's story. The good ones last. A waltz which you can like only when you are waltzing is a bad waltz.'

C.S. Lewis, 'On Three Ways of Writing for Children'

SINGLE NOVELS

☞ **Wizzy and Boa**
Anna Fienberg, illustrated by Ann James, Dent, 1988
(Australia). Ages 9-11 years. LIBRARY

Anna Fienberg's humour, like Lois Lowry's, is robust and charming; and her two main characters, Boadicea (Boa) and Ludwig van Weezelman (Wizzy), profit hugely from it. The book's plot, which involves imaginary pirates connected with Boa's grandfather, an Admiral, is not a sufficiently interesting vehicle for either of them. But snippets of adventure work. With a more compelling story line, Fienberg could emerge as one of our better comic writers for children. No doubt the judges who short-listed her for an Australian national award thought so, too.

☞ **The Story of Holly and Ivy**
Rumer Godden, illustrated by Barbara Cooney, Julia
MacRae, reprinted 1985 (original publication date 1957)
(England). Ages 8-9 years. LIBRARY, CHILD

All Rumer Godden's stories about dolls appeal enormously to a certain species of young girl. This one may well be the favourite of beginning readers, because its portrait of an orphan, lost during a snowstorm and friendless except for the doll she sees in a shop window just before Christmas, is as absorbing as its depiction of

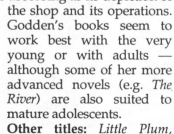

the shop and its operations. Godden's books seem to work best with the very young or with adults — although some of her more advanced novels (e.g. *The River*) are also suited to mature adolescents.

Other titles: *Little Plum, Tottie* and many others.

☞ *The Iron Man

*Ted Hughes, illustrated by George Adamson, Faber, 1968
(England). Ages 8-9 years.* LIBRARY, CHILD

'The Iron Man came to the top of the cliff. How far had he walked? Nobody knows. Where had he come from? Nobody knows. How was he made? Nobody knows. Taller than a house, the Iron Man stood at the top of the cliff, on the very brink, in the darkness. . . hearing the sea. His eyes, like headlamps, glowed white, then red, then infra-red, searching the sea.'

This is the start of Ted Hughes' unusually robust story about a creature who falls from a cliff, gets put together again, becomes part of a small community, presumably in England, and tames a monster that's landed in Australia and is threatening all humanity.

Other titles: Hughes' other books for children are poetry (e.g. *What is the Truth?*).

☞ Stig of the Dump

*Clive King, illustrated by Edward Ardizzone, Hamish
Hamilton, 1965 (England). Ages 8-10 years.* LIBRARY

Clive King's specialty is fantasy which dramatises the improbable: a town moving from England to Australia in a flood, or a young boy discovering his origins after years on the open sea. In *Stig of the Dump* Barney makes friends with a grunting creature in a rabbit skin, with shaggy black hair and bright black eyes, whose home is a cave at the bottom of his local chalk-pit.

Stig, it turns out, is no ordinary friend: he can do all kinds of marvellous things. He can draw splendid hunters on his cave walls, transform a stone into a weapon, help Barney to catch thieves, trap a leopard that's escaped from the zoo, make speeches in an unusual language of his own and much else. The source of his giftedness is a mystery resolved only through a large hint at the end of the story.

Young boys with secret hideaways will appreciate his exploits.

Other titles: *Ninny's Boat, The Town That Moved South* and others.

☞ Magnus Powermouse

Dick King-Smith, illustrated by Mary Rayner, Gollancz,
1982 (England). Ages 9-11 years. LIBRARY

Although some adults may find Dick King-Smith's
hyperbolic prose cloying at times, many children will
be charmed by his comic animal fantasies — like this
one about an extraordinary rodent named Magnus
Powermouse. Thinking that the build of their huge and
powerful son must be the result of something they ate,
Magnus's bemused parents don't know quite what to
make of him, and neither do other animals who
encounter him under less fortunate circumstances than
they do — the neighbourhood cat, for example, part of
whose tail he bites off. The more enterprising creatures
whom he meets, like Jim the Rat, make the most of him
— with unpredictable, often amusing results. Mary
Rayner's fine line drawings deserve special mention.
Other titles: *Daggie Dogfoot, The Sheep-Pig* (Guardian
Award, 1984) and others.

☞ *Mrs Frisby and the Rats of NIMH

Robert C. O'Brien, Lions, 1971 (USA). Newbery Medal,
1972. Ages 10-13 years. LIBRARY, CHILD, GENERAL

After she frees a crow entangled in a string so that he is
able to escape from the cat who wants him for dinner, a
mother mouse named Mrs Frisby is herself freed from
danger by this same crow, Jeremy. 'Just in time,' he
says, as he carries her on his back away from the cat.
'It's lucky you're so light. I can scarcely tell you're
there. . . I'll drop you off [at your front door].'

The concern and friendliness evident in this brief
encounter typify relations among all the animals in this
highly imaginative novel. O'Brien's central focus is the
pattern of communal life developed by a group of
educated, enormously intelligent rats who live
underneath a rosebush near Mrs Frisby's home.
Besides vowing to stop stealing so that they can no
longer be identified as a danger to the world, Justin,
Brutus, Nicodemus and their friends concoct an
elaborate plan designed to perpetuate their community

for generations. In its details, this plan is as impressive and endearing as the animals themselves.

Other titles: *The Silver Crown*. A sequel to *Mrs Frisby and the Rats of NIMH*, written after Robert O'Brien's death by his daughter, Jane Leslie Conly, and entitled *RACSO and the Rats of NIMH*, is available in Puffin.

☞ *Midnite

Randolph Stow, illustrated by Ralph Steadman, Puffin, 1967 (Australia). Ages 10-13 years. LIBRARY, CHILD

This book is unique: a witty satirical thrust at *Captain Starlight* which no young reader spots, but which appeals to a young audience just the same. Focussing on seventeen-year-old Midnite's many adventures, his battles with Trooper O'Grady, and his devoted train of five animals (especially Khat — cream coloured, with blue eyes and a coffee-coloured tail), Stow sends up the Australian bushranging tradition and much else.

Many children will respond to the book as a comic fable. Adults regard it as a classic, as irreverent as Dame Edna.

Other titles: Stow is known primarily as a writer for adults, but *The Merry-Go-Round in the Sea* can be read by mature adolescents of fifteen or older.

☞ *Charlotte's Web

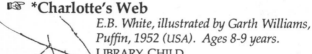

E.B. White, illustrated by Garth Williams, Puffin, 1952 (USA). Ages 8-9 years. LIBRARY, CHILD

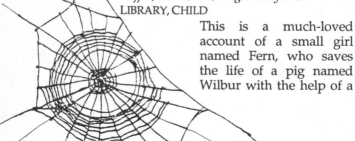

This is a much-loved account of a small girl named Fern, who saves the life of a pig named Wilbur with the help of a

marvellously clever spider called Charlotte. The inventiveness of Charlotte, the ingenuity of the plot and the vitality of the dialogue and of characters like Templeton the rat give White's story a unique charm. It can be read by young and middle primary children, or read aloud with great effect to younger children.

Typical of its tone is the following brief extract: 'This was almost more than Wilbur could stand: on this dreary, rainy day to see his breakfast being eaten by somebody else. He knew Templeton was getting soaked, out there in the pouring rain, but even that didn't comfort him.'

Other titles: *Stuart Little, Trumpet of the Swans.*

☞ *The Nargun and the Stars

Patricia Wrightson, Puffin, 1973 (Australia). Australian Children's Book of the Year, 1974. Ages 11-13 years.
LIBRARY, CHILD, GENERAL

Simon Brent, who comes to live with his elderly cousins Edie and Charlie in the Hunter Valley when his parents are killed in a car crash, finds companionship he never knew existed, and new reasons for being alive. His cousins — unconventional and highly imaginative people, very sensitive to Simon's situation — share his love for the natural world and his interest in the magical creatures who preserve it.

Among these creatures are a green spirit of the swamp called a Potkoorok, who talks to Simon and plays him all sorts of tricks; dancing tree spirits named Turongs, who attack road workers' equipment; and a lumbering, mysterious, stony figure as old as the earth called a Nargun. The difference they make to Simon and to Wongadilla is Wrightson's subject, and she handles it much less statically than she does related themes in later novels which also make use of Aboriginal myth and legend.

Other titles: *The Rocks of Honey, An Older Kind of Magic* and others.

SERIES

☞ Selby Speaks
Duncan Ball, illustrated by Allan Stomann, Angus and Robertson, 1988 (Australia). Ages 8-9 years. LIBRARY

This sequel to *Selby's Secret*, which won a Readers' Award in Western Australia in 1987, is about a talking dog who carefully refrains from speech in case such an oddity creates more difficulties for him than he has already. Like the first Selby book, this one recounts a series of amusing adventures, beginning with an episode in which a pink parrot threatens to give Selby away, and including an encounter with an acquisitive truck driver who hears the dog speak, demands that he give him 'proper English', not 'bow wow rubbish' so that he can get rich quick, and is given his comeuppance at the edge of a cliff from which Selby saves him (refusing to talk).

The pace is too rushed and the series as a whole is lightweight; but reluctant readers apparently find the short, packed chapters appealingly farcical.

Other titles in the series (so far): *Selby's Secret.*

☞ *The Mouse and the Motorcycle
Beverly Cleary, illustrated by Louis Darling, Dell, 1965 (USA). Ages 9-11 years. LIBRARY, CHILD

The winner of three children's awards for favourite book of the year, this novel, the second in a series, is about the secret friendship of a mouse named Ralph and a boy, Keith. They meet at the Mountain View Inn, where Keith is staying with his parents at the start of a three-to-four-week vacation. When Ralph confiscates Keith's toy motorcycle and begins riding it along the Inn's corridors, he is spotted. But instead of fireworks, a series of adventures takes place, including a disastrous crash by Ralph into a pillow case and his subsequent capture by other children staying at Mountain View. Typically, Beverly Cleary is full of surprises as she chronicles Ralph's and Keith's amusing escapades.

Other titles: *Ralph S. Mouse* and *The Runaway Mouse*.
Other series: *Ramona the Pest* (see p. 47), *Henry Huggins* and *Ribsy* (see p. 39).

☞ Marmalade and Rufus
Andrew Davies, illustrated by John Laing, Abelard, 1979 (England). Ages 8-9 years. LIBRARY

After winning two major awards for *Conrad's War*, a comic fantasy which teaches a young boy the difference between films and the real thing, Andrew Davies began writing a comic fantasy series about Marmalade Atkins, a girl who says rude things when she feels like it and does Bad Things when the urge hits her. In this, the first book in the series, Marmalade's adventures with her talking donkey, Rufus, land her in a nightclub, a midnight steeplechase and other forbidden territory. Throughout, her exploits are handled with a bemused irreverence well suited to beginning readers with an eye for farce.
Other titles in the series: *Educating Marmalade, Marmalade Atkins in Space, Marmalade Hits the Big Time* and many others.

☞ Finn Family Moomintroll
Tove Jansson, illustrated by Tove Jansson, Puffin, 1948 (Finland). Ages 9-11 years. LIBRARY, CHILD

Whether they are sleeping under the snow for the winter, playing hide and seek in spring, diving under tables, climbing on rocks or looking for reefs and islands, the Moomins — small, shy and fat, and at home in the forests of Finland — will appeal to a certain breed of eight- or nine-year-old. The adventures of the Snork Maiden, Snufkin, Sniff, and other creatures invented by Jansson can be recounted aloud to younger children or silently taken in by their older siblings. Some readers may find their shenanigans overly cute and affected; but many youngsters will be enthralled.
Other titles: *Comet in Moominland, Moominsummer Madness* and many others.

☞ *Tamworth Pig and the Litter

*Gene Kemp, illustrated by Carolyn Dinan, Faber, 1975
(England). Ages 9-11 years.* LIBRARY, CHILD

In this, the third book in Gene Kemp's amusing and inventive series about the irrepressible Thomas, his more reasonable sister Blossom and the talking creatures who enliven their lives, the focus is on two kinds of litter: Tamworth Pig's new progeny, and the rubbish polluting the village stream and duck pond. Although Tamworth complains that there is nothing to be seen in the neighbourhood except 'detritus', and though he works hard in the campaign to rid the area of it, he also is very good at doing other kinds of worthwhile things, like cheering up Thomas after a series of disappointments.

The great charm of the book for young readers entering its world for the first time is its nonchalant assumption that of course animals and dolls speak, and of course they exist for the benefit of children and adults as well as for their own.

Other titles in the series: *The Prime of Tamworth Pig, Tamworth Pig Saves the Trees, Christmas with Tamworth Pig.*

☞ *The Borrowers

Mary Norton, Puffin, 1952 (England). Carnegie Medal, 1952. Ages 10-12 years. LIBRARY, CHILD

This is the first book in a classic series about a tiny, fantastic family — Pod, Homily and their daughter Henrietta — who live in an orderly country house underneath a grandfather clock which has stood in its entrance hall for two hundred years. Their adventures, after they are discovered by a boy with rheumatic fever who comes to visit the mistress of the house, his great-aunt Sophy, are amusing and diverting. Children take an absorbed interest in them not unlike that revealed by this same boy's sister Kate, who tells their story years after he has become an adult.

Other titles in the series: *The Borrowers Aloft, The Borrowers Afield, The Borrowers Afloat, The Borrowers Betrayed.*

☞ The Indian in the Cupboard

Lynne Reid Banks, illustrated by Robin Jacques, Dent, 1980 (England). Ages 9-11 years. LIBRARY

Like Lynne Reid Banks's other novels, including those for older children, this one is uneven in quality, too reliant on cliché and gushy at times. But its central situation is intriguing.

A miniature plastic Iroquois Indian brave given to Omri by his best friend Patrick comes to life after being left in a cupboard overnight. Not only that: the same thing happens to every small plastic toy left in this same cupboard. Keeping these magical events secret from adults and controlling the behaviour of the live toys demand a lot of both children. Later books in the series create further adventures for the toys and the boys.

Other titles in the series: *The Secret of the Indian, The Return of the Indian.*

*Books for younger readers
(8 to 12 years)*

FANTASY:
*Quests/
Transformations*

'We live in an open, interacting, creative universe, and to try to close it into a safe little system is a danger to ourselves and a danger to everyone we touch. But if we are willing to be a small part of a great whole, then we know that no part in the dance is too small, too unimportant to make a difference.
We are all like the butterfly in the amazing, unexpected magnitude of our effect.'

Madeleine L'Engle, *A Stone for a Pillow*

SINGLE NOVELS

☞ *The Secret Garden

Frances Hodgson Burnett, Puffin, 1911 (England). Ages 10-12 years. LIBRARY, CHILD

Although this classic is well known, contemporary readers might easily dismiss it, unread, as too old-fashioned for the '90s. This would be a mistake. Its portraits of Mary Lennox, a self-centred orphan living next to a locked garden on her uncle's Yorkshire estate, and the persons who slowly bring her out of herself — Dickon a gardener and her sickly cousin Colin Craven, whom she in turn restores to health — are memorable and timeless. By the end of the book, the Mary with a headache who does her best to see that everyone else has a headache, and the Colin whose screaming tantrums shake the house, have been transformed by the magic of the secret rose garden which was once the refuge of Colin's mother.

☞ *The Haunted Mountain

Mollie Hunter, illustrated by Trevor Ridley, Lion, 1974 (Scotland). Ages 8-10 years. LIBRARY, CHILD

Always a superb story teller, Mollie Hunter outdoes herself in this tale about MacAllister, a handsome and stubborn man who defies the fairy folk (sidhe) known

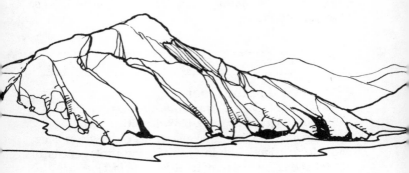

to control a piece of his land called Goodman's Croft. By cultivating this small plot of ground, he invites a series of disasters, the most terrible being his own, apparently interminable, incarceration inside a huge and terrifying mountain called Ben MacDui. In the end only his courageous son Fergus and their equally valiant dog Colm can hope to save him from permanent imprisonment in the domain of the Great Grey Man who stalks their haunted mountain.

Other titles: *The Kelpie's Pearls, The Enchanted Whistle* and many others.

☞ *Master of the Grove

Victor Kelleher, Puffin, 1982 (Australia). Australian Children's Book of the Year, 1983. Ages 11-13 years.
LIBRARY, CHILD, GENERAL

Many readers are unable to put down this haunting tale about a lame boy named Derin whose first difficult task is to find his missing father, captured by soldiers of the Citadel who destroy his upland farm. Additional tasks, equally tough, involve Derin with mountain people ruled by a Sacred Circle of the Grove and these same Citadel soldiers, who are governed by a Council at war with the mountaineers. An old woman, Marna, and her companionable raven, whom he meets early in the piece, help him throughout his arduous quest. Ultimately, his journey issues in self-discovery as well as exciting solutions to tangible practical dilemmas.

Other titles: *The Hunting of Shadroth, The Hidden Paths of Thual* and others.

SERIES

☞ *A Wind in the Door

Madeleine L'Engle, Farrar, Straus, and Giroux, 1973 (USA). Ages 10-13 years. LIBRARY, CHILD

The remarkable Charles Wallace, his older sister Meg, and Meg's friend Calvin O'Keefe, the protagonists of Madeleine L'Engle's famous *A Wrinkle in Time*, are also the major characters of its sequels. *In A Wind in the Door*, six-year-old Charles, plagued by bullies at school who resent his brilliance, develops a strange illness which his mother's scientific research sheds light on but cannot cure. Ultimately, his well-being depends on the combined efforts of his deeply intuitive sister Meg, his unlikely school principal Mr Jenkins (ostensibly a cold fish), Calvin and an assortment of well-wishers, some of them from distant parts of the galaxy. Altogether believably, Madeleine L'Engle invents a language and a mode of being for creatures engaged in a cosmic battle over human dignity. Concepts used in the novel, such as 'kything' (speaking without words, knowing another's wishes), become permanent reader acquisitions.

Other titles in the series: *A Wrinkle in Time* (Newbery Medal, 1963), *A Swiftly Tilting Planet* (American Paperback Award, 1980), *Many Waters.*

Other series: *Dragons in the Waters* (see p. 157), *A Ring of Endless Light* (see p. 119).

Part B

Books for older readers (12 to 15 years)

REALISM:
Coming of age

'Children are meant to grow up, and not to become Peter Pans. Not to lose innocence and wonder, but to proceed on the appointed journey: that journey upon which it is certainly not better to travel hopefully than to arrive, though we must travel hopefully if we are to arrive.'

J.R.R. Tolkien, 'Children and Fairy Stories'

SINGLE NOVELS

☞ The True Story of Lilli Stubeck

James Aldridge, Puffin, 1984 (Australia). Australian Children's Book of the Year, 1985. Ages 14-15 years.
LIBRARY, CHILD, GENERAL

When the down-and-out Stubeck family leaves their daughter Lilli behind in the country town of St Helen after a brief visit, nobody understands why a wealthy and strict single woman, Miss Dalgleish, 'buys' and tries to tame her. Lilli herself resists being owned by anybody. At every stage her battle to be her own person is absorbing, highly individual and instructive.
Other titles: *The Broken Saddle* (see p. 33), *The True Story of Spit MacPhee* (Guardian Award, 1987) and many others.

☞ A Kind of Wild Justice

Bernard Ashley, Oxford, 1978 (England). Ages 12-14 years. LIBRARY, CHILD

This novel was the runner-up for the 1978 Carnegie Medal, presumably because of Bernard Ashley's powerful descriptions of the terror experienced by a boy hounded by criminals with whom his father has been involved. Ronnie's fear and isolation aren't helped by his mother's leaving home, or the total lack of understanding he receives at school. His life is tough indeed — too tough, perhaps, to be altogether believable. Although we enter sympathetically into Ronnie's entire situation, the difficulties he faces are so constant and horrific that they seem at times fabrications — a form of special pleading.
Other titles: *Terry on the Fence, The Trouble With Donovan Croft* and other novels about lone boys facing modern forms of violence.

☞ *A Place to Come Back To

Nancy Bond, Atheneum, 1985 (USA). Ages 14-15 years.
LIBRARY

Set in historic Concord, Massachusetts, the town in which Nancy Bond was raised, *A Place to Come Back To* is chiefly about place. Where Oliver Shattuck, great-nephew of octogenarian Commodore Shattuck, is going to stay if and when the Commodore can no longer maintain him is the book's focal question.

Shunted from one boarding school to another, homeless while his parents fight and divorce, deeply at home at last with his great-uncle in his old Concord house, Oliver has no wish to rejoin his career-centred mother or her second husband. Despite the increasing complexity of his relations with his best friends Charlotte Paige and Andy and Kath Schuyler, he wants to stay put for as long as he possibly can.

Nancy Bond is superb on the network of personal ties and pressures impinging on Oliver and, what's best, she doesn't falsely tie up loose ends for the sake of structural neatness.

Other titles: *The Best of Enemies* (a prequel) and *A String in the Harp* (Newbery Honor Book 1977, see p. 143). Others are not available in Australia.

☞ The Goats

Brock Cole, illustrated by Brock Cole, Farrar, Straus, and Giroux, 1987 (USA). Ages 13-15 years. LIBRARY

This is a moving first novel about the friendship that develops between a teenage boy and girl, Howie and Laura, who have been rejected at a summer camp by their peers, stripped and left to their own devices on an abandoned island.

Cole's style is spare, strong, direct and assured. He manages shifts in emotional tone particularly well. But he also tells a good story. Experienced readers will know him because of his fine illustrations for books for younger children.

Other titles: Recently published in USA, to rave reviews: the over-rated *Celine*.

☞ Holding Me Here

Pam Conrad, Oxford, 1986 (USA). Ages 14-15 years.
LIBRARY

In elegant prose, Pam Conrad dramatises family situations whose painful unpredictability causes her adolescent heroines to take stock and grow by leaps. No subject for young people, however difficult — alcoholism and drug addiction within the family, a young mother's apparent abandonment of her children, uncontrollable male violence — scares her.

In *Holding Me Here*, her focus is the effect of parental separation upon fourteen-year-old Robin Lewis. Seeking family reunion, but acting out of hurts she does not understand, Robin interferes in the life of a boarder living in her mother's house. Only after she releases violence beyond her wildest imagining is she ready to hear her father on upside-down lives: 'Sometimes from the outside we think we can see what someone should do with their life, but we're not in that person's head. There's no way we can really ever know what someone has to do.'

Other titles: *Taking the Ferry Home, Prairie Songs* (an American Library Association Best Book set at the turn of the twentieth century) and others.

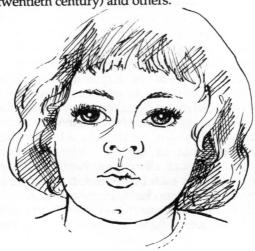

☞ Dear Shrink

Helen Cresswell, Puffin, 1982 (England). Ages 13-15 years. LIBRARY, CHILD

When their botanist parents take off for the Amazon on a study trip, leaving them in the care of 'a kindly soul' named Mrs Bartle who looked after their mother years before, Oliver, William and Lucy Saxon face difficulties undreamt of at the start of the venture. Barty's sudden death not only separates them; it places them at the mercy of a succession of temporary caretakers who make their lives a misery.

Their story is recounted in witty and gory detail by Oliver, who is thirteen when his parents leave for South America. Cresswell is trenchant on the forms of abuse unreasoning adults foist on children.

Other titles: *The Bongleweed* (for younger readers) and many others, including the zany Bagthorpe series which produces very mixed reactions in readers.

☞ The Inner Circle

Gary Crew, Heinemann, 1986 (Australia). Ages 13-15 years. LIBRARY

Gary Crew, for many years a high school English teacher in Brisbane, is a relative newcomer to children's writing. Although his first two novels have received deserved praise for their sympathetic portraits of troubled teenage boys, both — but especially his second — are significantly flawed in structure.

The first works better, despite its more conventional narrative, and appeals to reluctant as well as to more seasoned readers. It depicts the developing friendship of two isolated adolescents, Joe (Aboriginal) and Tony (white), as they struggle to make a life for themselves apart from, but in uneasy conjunction with, their families. Although alternating chapters fail to establish a clear voice for each boy narrator, the novel succeeds in involving readers closely in their worlds.

Other titles: *The House of Tomorrow. Strange Objects* just out. Australian Children's Book of the Year, 1991.

☞ Running Loose

*Chris Crutcher, Greenwillow, 1983 (USA). An American
Library Association Best Book. Ages 14-15 years.*
LIBRARY

Of the writers listed in this section of the guide (with
the possible exception of Gary Paulsen), Chris Crutcher
is most likely to appeal to reluctant readers, particularly
boys. His big subject is sport. But his novels also treat
other matters of substance — sexual longing, family life
(sometimes very difficult), worldly corruption and the
school of hard knocks — in a colloquial mode which
captures the flavour of the speech and values of
ordinary Americans extremely well. His major figures
are physically attractive, popular and robust, and —
even when they suffer extreme disappointment as
Louie Banks does in *Running Loose* — they battle on
courageously.

Crutcher tells their stories with warmth and energy,
and his view of life is coolly balanced. Although his
prose is often glossy and too much of his portraiture
(especially his girls) one-dimensional, the way he feels
about the tough situations he dramatises is bound to
make a strong impression on adolescents.

Other titles: *The Crazy Horse Electric Game* and *Stotan!*

☞ Village by the Sea

Anita Desai, Puffin, 1982 (India). Ages 14-15 years.
LIBRARY, CHILD, GENERAL

Like Anita Desai's novels for adults, this evocative
portrait of life in a village near Bombay and in the city
itself reveals as much about India as it does about
individual lives — though its depiction of a young and
impoverished brother and sister is absorbing. Many
older readers will find especially striking those urban
scenes in which twelve-year-old Hari's struggle to stay
alive under appalling circumstances is fully detailed.
Poverty on a scale unknown in the West is made real,
but so, too, is the beauty of Indian life.

☞ The Summer-House Loon

Anne Fine, Methuen, 1974 (England). Ages 14-15 years.
LIBRARY, CHILD, GENERAL

Anne Fine's unusual first novel, which was the runner-up for a Guardian award, shows how an adolescent girl named Ione Muffet comes to comprehend and influence the lives of the adults surrounding her. Although at first the remarks and activities of Ione's blind Professor father, his secretary Caroline Hope, and Caroline's allegedly loony suitor Ned Hump, a student of Professor Muffet's, make little sense to her, they eventually cohere. And when they do, in ways which are amusing to the point of farce, she is able to take command of her own life and, to a degree, theirs.

As with later Fine novels like *Madame Doubtfire*, in which farce figures prominently and very successfully, a mature intelligence is expected of readers.

Other titles: *Madame Doubtfire, Goggle Eyes* (Guardian Award and Carnegie Medal, 1990) and others.

☞ *One-Eyed Cat

Paula Fox, Dell, 1984 (USA). Newbery Honor Book. A Hans Christian Andersen Medal winner. Ages 12-14 years. LIBRARY, CHILD, GENERAL

The birthday rifle given to him by his uncle and consigned to the attic by his clergyman father and his arthritic mother involves Ned Wallis in lives he's known nothing significant about before. A secret shot in the dark, fired at a moving shadow, brings Ned the company of a taciturn, astute old man named Mr Scully,  the rambling countryside around his Hudson River Valley house, and a one-eyed wild cat native to the area. Their story, interspersed with an evocative account of life at Ned's father's isolated rural rectory, commands an unusual intensity of interest.

Other titles: *The Village by the Sea* (see p. 105), *The Slave Dancer* (Newbery Medal, 1974) and many others.

☞ All We Know

Simon French, Angus and Robertson, 1986 (Australia). Australian Children's Book of the Year, 1987. Ages 12-14 years. LIBRARY, CHILD, GENERAL

In his best book so far, Simon French captures the feel of life on a city street (Ramsay) dominated by tower blocks, and of the emotional ups and downs of a family living on it. His focus is on shifting personal relations: on his main character, Arkie's, ties with her mother and her de facto spouse (both teachers), her younger brother Jo, a once close friend, Kylie, her sixth class teacher, Mr Clifford, and especially a lonely boy from down the street, Ian.

Simon French approaches his characters' longings with an understated, almost remote clarity that appeals very strongly to those whose lives are confused and in flux.

Other titles: *Cannily, Cannily.*

☞ The Summer after the Funeral

Jane Gardam, Puffin, 1973 (England). Ages 14-15 years. LIBRARY, CHILD, GENERAL

The death of Athene Price's father engenders changes in the entire family, but especially in Athene herself as she is shunted from one household to another so that her mother can cope. Gardam's delineation of large, characteristic shifts in teenage emotion and awareness demands a lot of readers — especially, perhaps, non-British ones; but those who enter her universe easily find it endlessly funny, sad and interesting.

Typical of her manner is this brief extract from a conversation Sebastian, Athene's brother, has with a clergyman: 'I very much detested my father. . . He died in July and I am very glad he did. . . I imagine however that this is a sin. I want to know what to do about being glad about it.'

Other titles: *A Long Way from Verona, Bridget and William* (see p. 35) and others.

☞ *M.C. Higgins the Great

Virginia Hamilton, Lions, 1974 (USA). Newbery Honor Book, 1974 National Book Award, Globe-Horn Book Award, 1975. Ages 12-14 years. LIBRARY, CHILD

This is a beautifully written book about a young black boy, M.C. Higgins, who likes few things better than sitting high up on his steel pole surveying his surroundings in Appalachia. The trouble is that behind his family home among green mountains is an enormous strip mining slaghead which is slipping slowly downwards and threatening to wipe out everything the Higginses hold dear.

In the midst of potential disaster M.C. lives his life: he cherishes the hope that his mother will one day be a famous singer, becomes involved in a difficult and instructive friendship with a wandering, attractive young woman several years his senior (Lurhetta) and assumes neighbourhood responsibilities. On the closeness of the Higgins family, the importance of the natural world and enduring personal values, Hamilton is first-rate. Her mode is a poet's.

Other titles: *Sweet Whispers, Brother Rush* (Newbery Honor Book, 1983), *The Magical Adventures of Pretty Pearl* (see p. 152) and many others.

☞ Thunderwith

Libby Hathorn, Heinemann, 1989 (Australia). Ages 12-14 years. LIBRARY, CHILD, GENERAL

When Lara Ritchie comes to live with her father's second family after her mother's death, she is treated with extreme hostility by his wife, Gladwyn, and their oldest daughter, Pearl, even after the younger children come round. Although Hathorn's prose is sometimes hackneyed and rarely as imaginative as that of the finest children's writers, she handles Lara's response to adversity within the family and outside it with sensitivity and thoroughness. The more mystical features of Lara's experience — especially the soundings from her deceased mother which issue in an unusual friendship with a larger-than-life dog — push credence a bit far. But on the feel of domestic life, the countryside in northern New South Wales, dead ends in adolescence and adult life and bonds in unlikely quarters, the novel works well.

Other titles: *All About Anna* and picture books for younger readers.

☞ **Kes**

Barrie Hines, Puffin, 1968 (England). Ages 12-14 years.
LIBRARY, CHILD, GENERAL

Barry Hines' novel about Billy Casper's life in the north of England in the 1960s — his enormous difficulties with his mother and brother, his equally difficult life at school, his prospects when he leaves — is unremittingly grim. But Hines' evocation of Billy's love for the kestrel hawk which he finds in the woods and patiently trains is strong and encouraging.

On a rare occasion, Billy speaks about this process at school: 'You ought to have seen her. Straight as a die, about a yard off t'floor. An' t'speed! She came twice as fast as when she had t'creance on, 'cos it used to drag in t'grass an'slow her down. She came like lightnin', head dead still, an' her wings never made a sound, then wham! Straight upon to t'glove, claws out grabbin' for t'meat. . . I was that pleased I didn't know what to do wi' missen'.'

Nobody interrupts: Billy's audience, fictional and real, is glued.

☞ **Of Love and Death and Other Journeys**

Isabelle Holland, Dell, 1975 (USA). Ages 14-15 years.
LIBRARY, CHILD

Having spent the first fifteen years of her life travelling in Europe with her high-spirited mother and a succession of stepfathers, Meg Grant is suddenly forced, in Perugia, to stop everything and consider essentials. The related discoveries that her mother has cancer, that her father was not told of her existence when her parents divorced before she was born, and that her mother wants her to know her biological father despite being happily married for some years, jolt her into important recognitions about love, joy, freedom and death.

Characteristically, the depth of Isabelle Holland's treatment of unconventional, lonely people becomes apparent only gradually, as a certain breeziness of tone, in keeping with aspects of Meg's life, slowly fades and is transformed into a more balanced gravity.

Other titles: *Alan and the Animal Kingdom*, *The Man Without a Face* (a controversial portrait of homosexual attachment).

☞ Slake's Limbo
Felice Holman, Scribner, 1974 (USA). Ages 12-13 years.
LIBRARY

Slake is a homeless thirteen-year-old boy who seeks refuge from the streets of New York by spending one hundred and twenty-one days living in the subway. There he sells used newspapers to earn enough money to buy one ham sandwich per day, systematically explores the entire underground system, sleeps in a makeshift 'room' of his own in a tunnel, amuses himself by reading messages on the subway walls, gratefully accepts articles of clothing from a cleaning lady who buys papers from him, and accepts an offer to sweep up in the café that sells him his ham sandwich so that he can enjoy the luxury of a complete lunch and dinner, plus a few extras, each day.

Felice Holman's portrait of his dark existence, and the subway people whose small acts of kindness help him to surmount extreme privation, is as sympathetic as it is unusual.

Other titles: *The Future of Hooper Toote*, *The Cricket Winter* and others.

☞ Lottery Rose

Irene Hunt, Scribner, 1976 (USA). Ages 12-14 years.
LIBRARY

Although this book is not nearly so well known as Irene Hunt's prize-winning *Up a Road Slowly*, it is in its class. A delicate exploration of personal relations, it traces the slow awakening of a young boy named George Burgess, who is sent by a local court to live in a home for boys run by a sympathetic and sensible nun named Mary Angela.

Even Sister Mary Angela does not realise, at first, the extent to which Georgie has been physically battered by his mother and her boyfriend Steve. But once she glimpses his deeply scarred back, she sees to it that everything that can be done is done — as tactfully and sensitively as it can be — to bring him back to full life. Her task is difficult and Irene Hunt dramatises it with understated feeling.

Other titles: *Across Five Aprils*, *Up a Road Slowly* (Newbery Award, 1967).

☞ *A Sound of Chariots

Mollie Hunter, Lions, 1973 (Scotland). Ages 13-15 years.
LIBRARY, CHILD

This semi-autobiographical account of nine-year-old Bridie McShane's grief at the death of her father has a power to which few readers, adolescent or adult, fail to respond. Vivid descriptions of the Lowlands village in Scotland where Bridie grows up in the 1920s, life in the McShane family and episodes which propel Bridie into writing, characterise it.

Typical of its evocative reflections is this brief comment about an injury caused by the thorns of a brier rose: '. . .her gaze was caught and held by the deep, dark red of the drops of blood against her skin, and like a revelation it struck her that this was the way the blood ran, drop by drop, in her veins. This was the stuff that kept her alive. This *was* her life, these shiny red drops welling from her skin, and with the inescapable fact that she would die some day still beating in her brain she was suddenly seeing them with an acuteness of vision that made it seem as if a skin had been peeled from her eyes.'

Other titles: *The Stronghold* (Carnegie Medal, 1974; see p. 130) and many others, including *The Haunted Mountain* (see p. 93).

☞ A Separate Peace

John Knowles, Heinemann, 1959 (USA). William Faulkner Foundation Award. Ages 13-15 years.
LIBRARY, CHILD, GENERAL

Although this book became a best-seller in the early sixties, its depiction of friendships and conflicts in the lives of a group of boys at one of America's better preparatory schools, Devon, on the eve of World War II has not dated at all.

Especially strong is its portrait of an innocent and thoroughly charming athlete named Phineas, who spurs his classmates on to increasingly daring feats of physical courage. The envy Phineas inspires in other boys is closely related to dark emotions in the adult world beyond Devon. For good reason, the novel is still a favourite school text for pupils in the middle years of secondary school.

☞ *A Very Long Way From Anywhere Else

Ursula Le Guin, Puffin, 1976 (USA). Ages 13-15 years.
LIBRARY, CHILD

Although Ursula Le Guin is known chiefly for her fantasies and science fiction, she has also written very effective works of realistic fiction for adults and older children. Perhaps the best of them is this short yet memorable book about the friendship of an awkward, scientifically-minded seventeen-year-old, Owen Griffiths, and a talented composer slightly older than he is, Natalie Field.

The novel is especially good at showing, bit by bit, what builds confidence, trustworthiness and a solid sense of direction in young people who are unsure of their place in the world and with one another. It handles the delicate issue of Owen's awakening and immature sexuality with imagination and tact.

Other titles: *A Wizard of Earthsea*, quartet (see p. 157) and many other novels.

☞ Autumn Street

Lois Lowry, Lions, 1980 (USA). Ages 13-15 years.
LIBRARY, CHILD, GENERAL

Although this novel has an outspoken candour reminiscent of other, more comic works by Lois Lowry, it is much more sombre than her usual realistic fiction — including *Rabble Starkey*. Its focus is the relationship of a seven-year-old girl, Elizabeth, with the black woman, Tatie, who works as a cook in her grandfather's house, and Tatie's adventurous grandson, Charles.

Set at the start of World War II, it chronicles apparently ordinary events in the life of Elizabeth at home and at school in the small town, two states away from their New York home, where the family go to live while their father is fighting. The feelings it evokes are far from ordinary and connected with conditions in the world beyond Pennsylvania. On the subject of violent death, it is stark and disturbing.

Other titles: *Rabble Starkey* (Globe-Horn Book Award, 1987), the Anastasia Krupnik series (see p. 48) and other novels.

☞ *Memory

Margaret Mahy, Dent, 1987 (NZ). Ages 14-15 years.
LIBRARY, CHILD, GENERAL

Jonny Dart's efforts to come to terms with the past, and in particular the death of his beloved sister, introduce him to out-of-the-way characters who come to mean a great deal to him. Chief among them is a batty old lady named Sophie, whom he ends up looking after in her wreck of a house. Because she is suffering from a form of senile dementia, she is incapable of caring properly for herself.

Mahy's handling of Jonny's friendship with Sophie and his relations with others is quirky, sensitive, amusing and moving. She establishes his world so thoroughly that everything that happens in it, including the apparently humdrum, reverberates.

Other titles: *The Changeover* (Carnegie Medal,1984, see p. 153), *The Haunting* (Carnegie Medal, 1982) and others.

☞ So Much to Tell You. . .

John Marsden, McVitty, 1987 (Australia). Australian Children's Book of the Year, 1988. Ages 14-15 years.
LIBRARY, CHILD, GENERAL

This account of a fourteen-year-old girl's breakdown, silent withdrawal and recovery creates an unexpected intensity of interest — unexpected because its diary form, which at first seems gimmicky, allows Marsden to develop his story with a tact that assumes increasing power and strength. As fragments of Marina's life slowly settle into place, readers want to know more and more about each of them. Together, they comprise a whole of striking subtlety and depth.

Other titles: Marsden's other books for older readers — e.g. *The Great Gatenby*, *The Journey* — though interesting, are not nearly so well crafted as this one and they contain sexually explicit scenes which will worry some readers.

☞ *A Formal Feeling

Zibby Oneal, Gollancz, 1983 (USA). Ages 14-15 years.
LIBRARY, CHILD, GENERAL

After Anne has been home from boarding school for some days just before Christmas, her older brother Spencer remarks that she's acting as if she's surrounded by a moat. The metaphor is apt. Following the death of her mother, Anne encloses herself in a grief so forbidding that very little can touch her. Even when she's asked by her English teacher to write about Emily Dickinson's well-known poem about mourning, 'After great pain, a formal feeling comes,' she is unable to connect the poem and her own emotions in a way that will bring her release.

As in her other books about troubled states of mind, Zibby Oneal is penetrating on her heroine's emotional condition, the behaviour it issues in and the process she must go through in order to be whole.

Other titles: *In Summer Light* (Globe-Horn Book Award, 1986), *The Language of Goldfish* and others.

☞ *Bridge to Terabithia

Katherine Paterson, Avon, 1977 (USA). Newbery Medal, 1978. Ages 12-14 years. LIBRARY, CHILD, GENERAL

This account of friendship, love and death is so good that it is difficult to find a reader who fails to respond to it. Terabithia is the secret kingdom created by Leslie Burke so that she and her friend Jesse Aarons can have a place just for themselves which they can rule, unhampered by anyone who might irritate, wound or hassle them. There, and sometimes in more ordinary places like Jess's family's church, they make plans, imagine worlds and discuss matters large and small, amusing and grave. Paterson's touch is almost faultless.

Other titles: *Jacob Have I Loved, The Great Gilly Hopkins* (see p. 46) and others.

☞ *Hatchet

*Gary Paulsen, Bradbury, 1987 (USA). Newbery Honor Book, 1987. Ages 12-15 years.*LIBRARY

Gary Paulsen is a relative newcomer to children's literature whose novels deserve to be much better known outside America than they are. His subject is extreme adversity and his settings are usually farms, woods or isolated countryside.

Typically, his protagonists are young adolescents starting out in life, facing parental drunkenness, outrageous violence, the disintegration of the family, backbreaking physical labour, poverty, hunger — or a combination of all of these difficulties. But unlike more sensational writers such as S.E. Hinton, Paulsen always provides them with authentic alternatives to destruction. In *Hatchet*, thirteen-year-old Brian Robeson survives a plane crash and fifty-four solitary days in the Canadian wilderness. His battle for survival in a natural world red in tooth and claw yet unmistakably beautiful is engrossing.

Other titles: *Windkill, Dogsong* (Newbery Honor Book) and others.

☞ A Tide Flowing

Joan Phipson, Methuen, 1981 (Australia). Ages 14-15 years. LIBRARY, CHILD

The terrible isolation experienced by fourteen-year-old Mark Taylor after his mother falls, or jumps, from the family sailboat into the Tasman Sea is not relieved by the undemanding kindness of his paternal grandparents, with whom he comes to live in Sydney, or the half-hearted efforts to reach him made by his father and his new wife Cynthia, who finally visit him.

Only spirits who are solitary in the way that he is — an albatross whom he first sees on the night of his mother's death, and an eighteen-year-old paraplegic and her mother whom he gets to know on his walks to the school bus in Avalon — are able to touch and comfort him. His bond with them, and with the natural world with which they are closely associated, gives this stoic tale point and meaning.

Other titles: *The Boundary Riders, Hide Till Daytime* and others for both younger and older readers.

☞ Pelican Creek
Maureen Pople, University of Queensland, 1988 (Australia). Ages 14-15 years.
LIBRARY, CHILD, GENERAL

Although *Pelican Creek* is not as absorbing as Maureen Pople's first novel for young people and adults, *The Other Side of the Family*, its narrative structure is equally distinctive. Without warning, Pople shifts from the present to the past and back again, focussing in each case on the lives of a small group of closely attached people.

Her essential concern is with what lasts and, therefore, with the past's slow and imperfect disclosures. Her protagonist, fourteen-year-old Sally Matthews, and a plucky woman of an earlier day, Ann Bird, don't meet as similar characters would in many of the powerful time travel fantasies currently being written for older children, but their lives intersect in ways which create formidable surprises for Sally and for us.

Other titles: So far, *The Other Side of the Family*.

☞ *Home from Home
Susan Price, Faber, 1977 (England). Ages 14-15 years.
LIBRARY, CHILD

After being cajoled by an irritating teacher into being part of a group called the 'Active Christians', fifteen-year-old Paul Mentor, an avowed atheist known by his friends as Tormentor, finds that he so likes spending time with the old lady he's meant to look after, Mrs Maxwell, that he neglects everything else. Secretly, he visits her every day, tidies up her house, shops with her, takes her to the park to feed the pigeons, listens to her tales about the past, completes paintings left unfinished by her grandson — in short, changes her life by helping her to forget her rheumatism and her loneliness.

Because Susan Price is such a firm realist — so amusing, candid and exacting on Paul's life with his family, his friends and his teachers — her portrait of his unlikely friendship with his 'gran' is wholly believable and affecting. It's also, like her other widely praised books, highly original.

Other titles: *The Ghost Drum* (Carnegie Medal, 1987), *The Devil's Piper* (written when the author was sixteen, so uneven in quality) and others.

☞ A Candle for Saint Antony

Eleanor Spence, Oxford, 1978 (Australia). Ages 14-15 years. LIBRARY, CHILD

This account of the friendship of an ordinary Sydney schoolboy, Justin Vincent, and an unconventional Viennese migrant, Rudi Mayer, raises uncomfortable questions about homoeroticism. Although the novel is not as disturbing as Isabelle Holland's exploration of a related theme in *The Man Without a Face*, it does confront head-on the difficulties faced by two fifteen-year-old boys whose absorption with one another is excessive.

In the end, Justin leaves Rudi for his sister — too neat a bow to conventional morality, many readers feel. But the pressures facing both boys along the way are delineated with candour.

Other titles: *The October Child* (Australian Book of the Year, 1977), *Me and Jeshua* (see p. 65) and others.

☞ *Tell Me If The Lovers Are Losers

Cynthia Voigt, Fawcett Juniper, 1982 (USA). Ages 14-15 years. LIBRARY, CHILD

This superb view of life at a New England girls' college in the early 1960s is the finest of Cynthia Voigt's single novels. Besides depicting the relationships of three roommates in compelling detail, it presents with absolute fidelity a portrait of an era. Stanton's Dean, Miss Dennis, a professor of philosophy; the first-year volleyball team; the families of all three girls; literary discussions; and some of the more representative attitudes of the period are rendered with a fullness and intensity rare in fiction covering similar terrain.

There are, of course, memorable scenes and characters, and important moral issues — e.g. how culpable is the theft of a person's ideas? — are explored with Voigt's characteristic toughness and depth.

Other titles: *Dicey's Song* (see p. 120), *The Runner* and others.

SERIES

☞ *Ring of Endless Light

Madeleine L'Engle, Dell, 1980 (USA), Lion, 1988 (UK and Australia). Ages 13-15 years.

LIBRARY, CHILD and some Christian bookshops

The third and best book in L'Engle's first series about the Austin family takes its title from the poem by Henry Vaughan which begins, 'I saw eternity the other night/Like a great ring of pure and endless light,/All calm as it was bright'.

In keeping with the spirit of Vaughan's reflections on the ephemeral and the permanent, it treats large questions about life and death, meaning and purpose, harmony and disunity — but with L'Engle's usual earthiness, humour and balance. Whether her immediate subject is dolphins, the slow dying of a wise old man, or a young girl's friendship with an unstable boy, she involves her readers as only a handful of writers for this age group are able to do.

The soundness of her values is reflected in the strong quality of her prose and the broad range of situations which she explores. No single work but all of her books taken together disclose her gifts.

Other titles in the series: *Meet the Austins, The Moon By Night*.

Other series: *Dragons in the Waters* (see p. 157) and *A Wind in the Door* (see p. 94).

☞ Pennington's Seventeenth Summer

K.M. Peyton, Oxford, 1970 (England). Ages 13-15 years.
LIBRARY, CHILD

The first in a series of three books about a colourful, erratic, troubled and talented young pianist named Patrick Pennington, this account of the sometimes amusing, sometimes appalling events at home and at school which get Pat into trouble with the law, his teachers, his parents and other young people is the most successful work in the trilogy. Fast-moving and full of incident, yet not superficial in its handling of personal relations and the causes of youthful caprice and instability, the novel is also instructive for readers who are vaguely interested in both classical and folk music, but not very knowledgeable about either.

Other titles in the series: *The Beethoven Medal, Pennington's Heir*.

Other series by K.M. Peyton: The *Flambards* trilogy.

☞ *Dicey's Song

Cynthia Voigt, Lions, 1982 (USA). Newbery Medal, 1982. Ages 13-15 years. LIBRARY, CHILD, GENERAL

The second in a series of compulsively engaging books about the Tillerman family and their closest friends, this novel centres on Dicey's gradual adjustment to life on her grandmother's rundown farm in rural Maryland. With her younger brothers, James and Sammy, and her younger sister Maybeth, she comes to accept and love her touchy maternal grandmother, and to value almost everything about the spiney way of life which has given the Tillermans their distinctive character. Whether she is battling her English teacher, working on her boat, earning money by working at Millie's local shop, or visiting her dying mother in Boston, Dicey tackles whatever is before her with relentless spirit and determination.

Voigt's prose is spare and taut, without ever being shackled by a natural restraint. Everything she touches has an authentic feel. As well as creating a family circle in which every reader feels completely at home, she has invented a world of her own which countless admirers consider theirs.

Other titles in the series: *Homecoming, A Solitary Blue, The Runner, Come a Stranger, Sons From Afar, Seventeen Against the Dealer.*

Books for older readers (12 to 15 years)

REALISM:
Historical adventure/
Personal relations

'Every book begins with questions. How must it have seemed to the people who lived through this experience? What choices would I have made in their place?
I must find the answers by going back in the past, by living side by side with them until the world they lived in becomes as real to me as the room in which I am working.'

Elizabeth George Speare, 'Laura Ingalls Wilder Award Acceptance Speech'

SINGLE NOVELS

☞ Young Mark

E.M. Almedingen, illustrated by Victor G. Ambrus,
Oxford, 1967 (USSR). Ages 13-15 years.
LIBRARY. A non-fiction book.

To develop his marvellous singing voice and to escape
from an unsatisfactory family life, an arranged
marriage and vocation, and endless hours of work on
his father's land, young Mark Poltoratzky leaves the
Ukraine in the mid 1740s and runs away to St
Petersburg.

E.M. Almedingen's account of Mark's adventures,
based on her great-great-grandfather's disorganised
notebook entries, reveals a great deal about his part of
the world and the people he meets on his travels.
Among the more striking events described are a storm
that almost kills him, his long stay with the monks who
save him and teach him to read, rescue in Moscow by a
generous old peasant woman, an attack on the road by
brigands and a dreamlike meeting with the teacher he
seeks.

Other titles: *Frossia, Anna* and others.

☞ Under Goliath

Peter Carter, Oxford, 1977 (England). Ages 13-15 years.
LIBRARY

When thirteen-year-old Alan Kenton's older brother
Billy is asked what's wrong with Northern Ireland, he
says: 'There's parts of this country where you can't get
a council house unless you're a Protestant. . . There are
parts of it where your votes are swindled to make sure
that the Catholics don't run it, even if they are in a
majority like Derry. . . And there are places where a
man can't get a job if he's a Catholic.'

In this strife-ridden country, in Belfast in 1969 where
a huge crane named Goliath overlooks the city, Alan
battles to remain his own person. Because he can't take
sides in any crude way, he is accused more than once of

treachery: by the rough Prods on 'his' side; the Catholic boy, Fergus Riley, whom he secretly befriends; Billy, who wrongly thinks he's become a Protestant extremist; and violent men and boys on both sides.

Peter Carter's portrait of Alan's world, and in particular his difficult friendship with Fergus, is admirably solid. It's a pity that this book, and others by him, are not easier to come by.

Other titles: *The Sentinels* (Guardian Award,1980), *The Black Lamp* and others.

☞ Ride the Iron Horse

Marjorie Darke, illustrated by Michael Jackson, Lions, 1973 (England). Ages 12-14 years. LIBRARY, CHILD

Marjorie Darke's prose can be hackneyed, and features of her plots strain credibility. But she is good at involving readers in the emotions of characters striving to better themselves.

In this novel about the huge changes facing a farming community in Britain after the invention of the

steam engine, she concentrates on the fortunes of young John Gate, who is torn between his desire to be a railway engineer and his loyalty to family and friends tenacious in their resistance to the coming of the railroad. On John's attachment to Frances, the daughter of the local squire, who secretly teaches him to read, and the trials he suffers as he moves up in the world, the book is absorbing, if at times overheated.

Other titles: *The Star Trap* (a sequel), *A Question of Courage* and others.

☞ *Granny Was a Buffer Girl

Berlie Doherty, Lions, 1986 (England). Carnegie Medal, 1987. Ages 14-15 years. LIBRARY, CHILD

At eighteen, Jess is told family secrets as interesting to the novel's readers as they are to her, secrets which disclose the meaning of her mother's enigmatic remark about her mother's sudden death: 'Now we've another life to celebrate.' As well as learning about her living Granny Dorothy, her husband Albert and their progeny, Jess enters the young lives of her own parents and her mother's father and mother, Jack and the deceased Bridie, beginning with their courtship and elopement under trying circumstances.

Because Berlie Doherty is a superb storyteller, what could be an ordinary family chronicle becomes a compressed, absorbing history of very much more. At its centre is the story of Jess's retarded younger brother, Danny, who dies young.

Other titles: *Tough Luck, How Green You Are!* and others.

☞ The Fire-Raiser

Maurice Gee, Puffin, 1986 (NZ). Ages 13-15 years. LIBRARY, CHILD

Although this novel is set in a New Zealand town in 1915, it is less a period piece than a slightly seedy slice of life. Since the identity of the man responsible for setting fires in his home town is revealed early, what he will do next and how much damage will be caused before he is caught are the questions which give the story its impetus.

As in other books by Gee, touches of melodrama alternate with well-judged renderings of the daily round. Notably effective are scenes of schoolboys swimming in a river which hosts violence at other times, adults threatening to attack a talented local music teacher who happens to be German, and children slowly uncovering the secrets of the fire-raiser.

Other titles: *The Halfmen of O, Under the Mountain,* and other fantasies or mysteries for older and intermediate readers.

☞ Summer of My German Soldier
Bette Greene, Hamish Hamilton, 1973 (USA). Ages 12-14.
LIBRARY, CHILD

Although the last section of this novel about the effect of a newly built German prison camp on a group of townspeople in Jenkinsville, Arkansas, during World War II contains embarrassingly melodramatic elements, the story Greene tells has power. Her portraits of a courageous and unconventional twelve-year-old Jewish girl, Patty Bergen, the black Nanny who mothers her, her odious parents, the Nazi prisoner whom she befriends and loves, and her bigoted home town raise questions about perennial spiritual issues.

It is easy to see why a significant number of Australian junior secondary schools, and in particular schools with special programs in religious education, use it as a text.

Other titles: *Get On Out of Here, Philip Hall* (see p. 22), *Philip Hall Likes Me, I Reckon Maybe* and others.

☞ The Wool-Pack
Cynthia Harnett, illustrated by Cynthia Harnett, Puffin, 1951 (England). Carnegie Medal, 1951. Ages 12-14 years. LIBRARY, CHILD

Life in fifteenth century England is re-created in this original tale about the only child of a Cotswold wool merchant, Nicholas Fetterlock, who is betrothed by family arrangement to Cecily Bradshaw, has a host of adventures, and eventually exposes the criminal actions of two wicked Lombards visiting his part of the world.

Many daily activities — shooting with the crossbow and longbow, weaving, dyeing cloth, attending high Mass, going to a country fair, taking long horse rides, playing stool ball, watching religious processions, overseeing shearing — are vividly described. But it is always Harnett's story that is of the first importance.

Other titles: *The Great House, The Writing on the Hearth* and others.

☞ The Endless Steppe
Esther Hautzig, Puffin, 1968 (USSR). Ages 12-14 years. LIBRARY, CHILD. A non-fiction book.

Esther Rudomin's family is arrested by the Russians and transported from Poland to Siberia when she is ten years old. *The Endless Steppe* tells the story of their five-year exile. Many of its details are unforgettable.

Years after reading the book, I remembered Esther washing her hair with clay, battling the wind on the Siberian steppe, hunting for more food, smearing goose fat on face, fingers and toes as protection against frostbite, and slowly knitting a red sweater in the freezing cold.

Other events in Esther's life, important as they are — for example, reading Turgenev, Chekhov and Dickens, or falling in love, at fifteen, with a schoolboy named Yuri — pale in comparison with these episodes of pain, rooted in courage and hope.

☞ *Isaac Campion
Janni Howker, Julia MacRae, 1986 (England). Ages 13-15 years. LIBRARY, CHILD

Of the talented young writers who have claimed international attention in recent years, Janni Howker is the most exciting. Her books are distinctive in structure and style, powerfully observant, direct, intense and muscular, earthed in British history, especially working class history.

In *Isaac Campion*, in only eighty-four pages, she tells the story of a man and his vanished world. Isaac is the son of a horse dealer, forced at the age of twelve, in 1900, to come to terms with the suffocating demands made by his father when his older brother Dan is killed in a freak accident. Before he is even an adolescent, his entire life is at stake.

Using Isaac as narrator, Howker raises and answers vital questions about family, work, the natural world, violence and recrimination, and justice; and she does so with a compressed flair and strength which one associates more with a poet like Seamus Heaney than with children's novelists.

Other titles: So far, *The Nature of the Beast*.

☞ *The Stronghold

Mollie Hunter, Lions, 1974 (Scotland). Carnegie Medal, 1975. Ages 14-15 years. LIBRARY, CHILD

The Stronghold tells the story of Coll, the eighteen-year-old foster son of Nectan, ruler of a tribe living in the Orkney Islands when the ancient Romans were travelling the seas seeking captive slaves. It is his duty to protect his island, which means that he must come to terms with rivalries, violence and obtuseness within his tribe as well as in its would-be conquerors.

Typically, Mollie Hunter depicts hidden and naked passions with strength and intensity. She is at her best in treating the spiritual dimensions of mystery and fate, love and sacrifice. But her account of how the defensive fortresses at the Orkneys, the brochs, came into being is also wonderfully inventive.

Other titles: *A Sound of Chariots* (see p. 111), *The Haunted Mountain* (see p. 93) and others.

☞ The Road From Home

David Kherdian, Julia MacRae, 1979 (Armenia).
Newbery Honor Book, Globe/Horn Book Award for
Non-Fiction. Ages 13-15 years.
LIBRARY, CHILD. A non-fiction book.

When the Turks begin systematic persecution of the Armenians in 1915, Veron, her family and her friends leave home seeking safety, but finding a succession of dangers. Kherdian's non-fictional account of their entire way of life — their customs, their values and the threats to it posed by barbarians — will fascinate adults as well as more youthful readers. The hardships all of the Armenian families travelling together endure — including, of course, sudden death — are dramatised with a graphic matter-of-factness impossible not to respond to with sympathy and horror.

☞ Goodnight Mister Tom

Michelle Magorian, Puffin, 1981 (England). Guardian
Award, 1982. Ages 12-14 years.
LIBRARY, CHILD, GENERAL

Despite some melodrama in the second half, Michelle Magorian's novel about a pathetically neglected nine-year-old, Willie Leech, a London evacuee who is sent to the country to live with a widower, Tom Oakley, during World War II, provides a host of pleasures for eager readers. Not the least of them is its evocation of rural life and the inhabitants of the village of Little Weirwold who, little by little, make a different boy of Willie.

Although *Goodnight Mister Tom* is longer than most books written expressly for children, the story it tells is absorbing enough to hold even the most inveterate addicts of short fiction, if they relish the printed word.
Other titles: *Back Home.*

☞ The Cabby's Daughter

David Martin, Hodder and Stoughton, 1974 (Australia).
Ages 13-15 years. LIBRARY

The turn-of-the-century battles of a teenage girl, Bess, who wants to live decently with her father in Mayhill, a former gold town in the Australian bush, are recounted in this novel, the most effective of David Martin's books for children. Bess's relations with her family, especially her grandmother; her efforts to keep alive the memory of her mother; her friendship with Wattie, the son of the town's prison warder; and much else give this period piece colour and vitality.

Other titles: *Hughie, The Chinese Boy* and others.

☞ Deepwater
Judith O'Neill, Hamish Hamilton, 1987 (Australia).
Ages 12-15 years. LIBRARY, CHILD, GENERAL

Life in a country town in northeastern Victoria during World War I is the subject of Judith O'Neill's second children's novel. Painstakingly, she shows us how ordinary Australian farming families were affected by events taking place thousands of miles away.

In the absence of young men, able girls like the book's narrator, fourteen-year-old Char, find themselves lambing, dipping, hay-making, chaff-cutting, butter-churning and picking walnuts and apples instead of completing their schooling. And families with German names — in this novel, the Henschkes, who are no longer even able to speak the language of their ancestors — are rejected in increasingly painful ways. On the more lamentable extensions of the war's brutal consequences, O'Neill is graphic indeed.

Other titles: *Stringybark Summer.*

☞ *The Exeter Blitz
David Rees, Hamish Hamilton, 1978 (England).
Carnegie Medal, 1978. Ages 12-14 years.
LIBRARY, CHILD

The effects of the 1942 bombing of Exeter on those who survived it is David Rees' fascinating subject. Taking one family, the Lockwoods, and their friends and neighbours, he sketches in essential features of their ordinary lives and shows exactly how everything is thrown topsy-turvy when the German bombs fall.

In Rees' handling of the minutiae of wartime there is scarcely a detail that isn't both credible and interesting. The exact feel of the era, the town, the people living there is beautifully caught. Not only are invented figures like the book's main character, fourteen-year-old Colin Lockwood, vividly rendered, but particular spots in which they run for shelter are; and Exeter Cathedral, in all its remarkableness, is presented almost live to those of us who've never seen

it. Having Colin at the Cathedral tower when the planes come is a masterful touch.
Other titles: *Waves*, *Risks* and others.

☞ A Pocket Full of Seeds
Marilyn Sachs, illustrated by Ben Stahl, Doubleday, 1973 (USA). Ages 12-14 years. LIBRARY

On the nature of anti-Semitism, and its effect on the lives of ordinary Jewish families living in Europe during World War II, Marilyn Sachs is instructive for bright intermediate, as well as older, readers. Through Nicole Nieman, whose comings and goings she depicts in a series of vignettes covering a six-year period — 1938 to 1944 — she shows what change is, and what it does. The results of the immense upheaval effected by Hitler are reflected in Nicole's shifting attitudes towards her parents and her sister, her parents' friends, her schoolmates and teachers, and life itself.

Like Sach's most effective books for younger readers — e.g. *Veronica Ganz* — the novel is strong on the forms resourcefulness takes in plucky youngsters, and it makes it very clear that leaps in inner growth are taken only by a minority.
Other titles: *A Summer's Lease*, *Class Pictures* and others.

☞ The Red Towers of Granada

Geoffrey Trease, illustrated by Charles Keeping, Puffin, 1966 (England). Ages 12-14 years. LIBRARY

Banished from the church and society for being falsely diagnosed as a leper, saved by a talented Jewish doctor named Solomon of Stamford who takes him with his family from England to Spain to try to find a medicine to heal Queen Eleanor, sixteen-year-old Robin of West wood has adventures which put to the test his best qualities.

Typically, through the dangers faced by his attractive young protagonist, Geoffrey Trease teaches readers a great deal about the history of a particular period — in this case, the late thirteenth century — at the same time that he entertains them thoroughly. Corruption in the church, the nature and effects of anti-Semitism in medieval Britain, the state of medical knowledge in 1290, and the look and feel of famous places like Cordova and Granada are some of the subjects Trease handles in passing as he dramatises Robin's entry into manhood.

Other titles: *The Field of the Forty Footsteps, The Crown of Violet* and others.

☞ *A Parcel of Patterns

Jill Paton Walsh, Kestrel, 1983 (England). Ages 14-15 years. LIBRARY, CHILD

In 1665, the villagers of Eyam in Derbyshire caught the Plague from a parcel of patterns sent from London. This splendid novel shows their responses to this calamity, focussing on a young girl named Mall Percival and all of the people in her life threatened by imminent death. We witness their attachments, their working lives, their quarrels, their varying strategies for dealing with the unprecedented and, above all, their strength of spirit. In barely more than a hundred pages, making use of details from the history and traditions of Eyam, Jill Paton Walsh recreates far more than a village, and also more than a fragment of Plague history. Her narrative structure is particularly impressive.

Other titles: *Gaffer Samson's Luck* (see p. 27), *Unleaving* and many others.

☞ The Machine-Gunners
Robert Westall, Puffin, 1975 (England). Ages 13-15 years. Carnegie Medal, 1975. LIBRARY, CHILD

When, in the middle of World War II, fifteen-year-old Chas McGill and his friends secretly build a bunker holding a stolen machine gun, they don't expect to be involved in serious war games — not in suburban Garmouth. But they are: partly because the adults they know are so out of touch with their activities, and partly because Westall shows war to be grotesquely unpredictable. Before Chas and the others can do anything about it, a German soldier enters their world and plays an increasingly large and unforeseen part in it. Westall's scenario is chilling indeed, but powerful and convincing.

Other titles: Other Westall books that I've tried to read have been grim to the point of distastefulness, and without this novel's strengths.

SERIES

☞ Bridle the Wind
Joan Aiken, illustrated by Pat Marriott, Cape, 1983 (USA). Ages 14-15 years. LIBRARY, CHILD

Like many of Joan Aiken's intricately designed novels, *Bridle the Wind* is set in the nineteenth century and combines realism and fantasy, melodrama and history. For me this combination strains credence, though for many readers it works well. In this, the second of Aiken's Felix Brooke series, fifteen-year-old Felix is shipwrecked in the Bay of Biscay on the way to visit his grandfather in San Sebastian. The monks who take him in on the island of St Just de Seignaux figure prominently in the book, long after he leaves them.

Their abbot, it seems, is mad; but the full story of his madness is not disclosed until the end of Felix's journey

through France and Spain. Also disclosed is the full
identity of the fifteen-year-old, Juan, who accompanies
him on his wanderings and to whom, despite their
quarrels, he becomes very attached.
Other titles in the series: *Go Saddle the Sea*, *The Teeth of
the Gale*
Other series: The Dido Twite books: *Black Hearts in
Battersea*, *Night Birds on Nantucket* and *The Stolen Lake*.

☞ When Hitler Stole Pink Rabbit
*Judith Kerr, illustrated by Judith Kerr, Collins, 1971
(England). Ages 12-14 years.* LIBRARY, CHILD

In 1933, when it was possible for Jews to escape from
Hitler's Germany without major harrassment, Anna
and Max were taken to Switzerland, France and finally
England by their parents with almost no prior warning.
Their father, a writer forbidden to publish in his native
land, had to start all over again — which meant that the
family had to get used to living in obviously straitened
circumstances.

Judith Kerr's largely autobiographical novel is
informative about what it meant to be displaced in such
an extraordinary way, and what gave families like hers
hope and strength. Everyday events in Anna's life,
such as learning a new language, adjusting to a foreign
school and trying to make new friends while remaining
in contact with people at home, are vividly recalled
with humour as well as appropriate gravity.
Other titles in the series: *The Other Way Round*, *A
Small Person Far Away*.

☞ The Twelfth Day of July
Joan Lingard, Puffin, 1970 (Ireland). Ages 12-14 years.
LIBRARY, CHILD

This is the first book about Kevin and Sadie, a young
couple who are unwilling to part despite the fact that
they dramatise in their own persons the conflict
between Protestants and Catholics disfiguring
Northern Ireland. On the feel of life in Belfast in the
late sixties, and on attitudes towards violence and

tradition held by ordinary people and dating back much further, Lingard is convincing and absorbing. But her books don't render character with the depth achieved by the very best writers. She's best on situations and their consequences.

Other titles in the series: *Across the Barricades, Into Exile, A Proper Place* and *Hostages to Fortune.*

☞ *Roll of Thunder, Hear My Cry

Mildred D. Taylor, Puffin, 1976 (USA). Ages 12-14 years.
LIBRARY, CHILD

The first in a series of at least three books about the Logan family, this moving exploration of nine-year-old Cassie's growing awareness of the meaning of skin colour in Mississippi in the 1930s also provides impressive portraits of family life and community relations among a closely knit group of black people. Powerful scenes give readers unfamiliar with southern American black social history a solid grasp of its salient features.

No-one who reads the series attentively can fail to understand what a family friend, Mr Morrison, means when he comments on the murder ot his parents, years before, by the Ku Klux Klan: 'Some folks tell me I can't remember what happened that Christmas — I warn't hardly six years ol' but I remembers all right. I makes myself remember.' Memory, Mildred D. Taylor makes clear, is a necessary aspect of justice and a means of preserving essential human ties.

Other titles in the series: *Let the Circle Be Unbroken, Song of the Trees* (for younger children).

☞ *The Iron Lily

Barbara Willard, Longmans, 1973 (England). Guardian Award, 1974. Ages 13-15 years. LIBRARY, CHILD

'Hard we lived and hard he died and hard I've lived wi'out him.' This remark, made by a servant girl near the end of Barbara Willard's sixth Mantlemass novel, applies to more than one life story in the series. Its most obvious application is to the lives of Lilias Rowan and her mother, who bring up children alone after the premature deaths of their hard-working husbands.

How they manage — especially, how Lilias manages — makes for fascinating reading, both because the sixteenth century world in which they live is evoked with such colour and fullness, and because their own grit is so powerfully rendered. An unresolved genetic mystery in Lilias' background gives the family saga another, more dramatic, dimension.

Other titles in the series: *The Lark and the Laurel, The Sprig of Broom, The Eldest Son, A Cold Wind Blowing, A Flight of Swans.*

Books for older readers (12 to 15 years)

FANTASY:
Time travel

'Fantasy differs from the stories of reality not in. . . drama, vitality, vividness, humor, dignity and truth to childhood, but in its imaginative virtuosity — the tossing up of ideas like brilliant balls of the most dazzling color and variety.'

Eleanor Cameron, *The Green and Burning Tree*

SINGLE NOVELS

☞ A String in the Harp

*Nancy Bond, Atheneum, 1976 (USA). Newbery Honor
Book, 1977. Ages 14-15 years.* LIBRARY

Nancy Bond's first novel dramatises the experience of a twelve-year-old boy named Peter Morgan, whose father takes him and his younger sister Becky to Wales to live after the death of their mother. When their fifteen-year-old sister Jen arrives for a visit from Massachusetts, she is drawn against her will into the world Peter inhabits.

In its daily forms this world is desolate. In its fantastic form, it is alive with meaning and interest. Through a magic key that he finds, Peter escapes from the terrible loneliness which afflicts him in his new home by entering imaginatively into the Welsh realm inhabited by a figure from Celtic mythology, the sixth century bard Taliesin. What he discovers there, and how he handles it, are the central concerns of the story.
Other titles: So far, *The Best of Enemies* and *A Place to Come Back To* (see p. 102).

☞ *The Court of the Stone Children

*Eleanor Cameron, Dutton, 1973 (USA). National Book
Award, 1974. Ages 12-15 years.* LIBRARY

At the art museum in San Francisco where she is working for the summer, Nina responds to carved stone figures in its courtyard in a manner that allows her to enter their lives, to discover key facts about a mystery unresolved in Napoleon's day and to connect past, present and future in essential ways.

Besides telling a fascinating and suspenseful story, Eleanor Cameron raises fundamental questions about the nature of imagination, the means by which we know other times and places, the operations of Time and the imperious demands of perennial, ungovernable passions. On Art as a powerful unifying force in individual lives and the history of the race, she is especially good.

Other titles: *To the Green Mountains* (runner-up, National Book Award, 1975), *That Julia Redfern* (see p. 28) and others.

☞ *The Root Cellar
Janet Lunn, Heinemann, 1981 (Canada). Canadian Children's Book of the Year, 1982. Ages 12-15 years.
LIBRARY

This blend of realism, fantasy and history is reminiscent of Eleanor Cameron, Ruth Park and Philippa Pearce, because it evokes an earlier time — the American Civil War period — with a devotion and tenderness which capture readers as fully as the character who travels back there. Twelve-year-old orphan Ruth Larkin's journey to find a missing soldier in the America that existed a hundred years earlier is exciting and moving, both because of its revelations about the War as Canadians and Americans experienced it, and because of its impact upon Ruth's present.

Like all the best time travel fantasies, it dramatises the importance of roots — familial, historical — and their connection with a release which allows love to develop and flourish.

Other titles: *Shadow in Hawthorn Bay*, *Double Spell* (for younger readers) and others.

☞ *A Pack of Lies
Geraldine McCaughrean, Oxford, 1988 (England). Carnegie Medal, 1988; Guardian Award, 1989. Ages 14-15 years. LIBRARY, CHILD

This is a brilliant book on the nature of fiction. Impossible to classify, it resembles a Chinese box because it contains stories within stories, some of which violate the ordinary conventions governing time and space. The stories themselves are fables: all have a moral — they are warnings to the people who hear them. But, like the tales told in the Arabian Nights, they may appear at first to be mere entertainments: strong in plot, romantic, magical — a pack of lies.

The storyteller in the novel, at its most realistic level, is a young man named M.C.C. Berkshire who appears out of nowhere in a library and comes to live and work at an antique shop owned by a widow, Mrs Povey, and her daughter Ailsa. When people come into the shop, instead of making an immediate sale, he regales them with a story which brings Mrs Povey more money than she could possibly have got in any other way. Who M.C.C. is, where he really comes from and much more about him remains a mystery until the end. Geraldine McCaughrean is an enchantress.

Other titles: So far, *A Little Lower Than the Angels* (Whitbread Award, 1987), *The Maypole*.

☞ The Lightning Time
Gregory Maguire, Harper and Row, 1983 (USA). Ages 12-14 years. LIBRARY

Gregory Maguire is a young writer who creates characters and plots with inimical features, and speaks clearly and engagingly in his own voice. So far, however, despite worthy concerns and linguistic inventiveness, he hasn't written a novel that entirely works. Typically, his fictional worlds alternate between being fully realised and hazily, stiffly or statically conceived, so that parts of his books are convincing and others have a concocted feel.

Though his most recent novel is available in our libraries, I prefer the first of his novels with an environmental theme, *The Lightning Time*. Suitable for upper primary and lower secondary readers, it focuses on the threat to a town in the Adirondack Mountains posed by a greedy developer, and the response to that threat offered by a visiting twelve-year-old boy and his mysterious 'cousin' Carrie, who belongs to an earlier time.

Other titles: *I Feel Like the Morning Star*, *The Dream Stealer* and others.

☞ Earthfasts

William Mayne, Puffin, 1966 (England). Ages 12-15 years. LIBRARY, CHILD

In a fantasy which places demands on many readers, an extra-ordinary candle connects the lives of King Arthur and his knights, an eighteenth-century drummer boy, called Nellie Jack John, and two modern English boys, David Wix and Keith Heseltine. As well, the candle dramatises fundamental differences in outlook — scientific and poetic — displayed by the two twentieth-century boys. Questions raised by William Mayne about the nature of knowledge and the means by which it is acquired will appeal to speculative older children. Others will probably be less interested than their parents — a continuing problem with Mayne's unusual and highly original books.

Other titles: *A Game of Dark, Royal Harry* and many others.

☞ *Playing Beatie Bow

Ruth Park, Puffin, 1980 (Australia). Australian Children's Book of the Year, 1981. Ages 12-14 years. LIBRARY, CHILD, GENERAL

Fourteen-year-old Abigail Kirk is self-centred and difficult to live with, chiefly because she is unable to come to terms with her parents' separation. When, through a miracle of time travel, she enters the lives of the Bow family, who lived in her part of Sydney — the Rocks — a century earlier, she falls in love and comes to understand and sympathise with her mother in a much more mature fashion. She also learns a great deal — as we also do — about Australian life one hundred years ago.

Of all of Ruth Park's esteemed books for children, this is the favourite of countless young people and adults: moving, suspenseful and fascinating.

Other titles: *Come Danger, Come Darkness, My Sister Sif* and many others.

☞ A Traveller in Time

Alison Uttley, illustrated by Faith Jacques, Puffin, 1939
(England). Ages 12-14 years. LIBRARY, CHILD

This is the first well-known book for teenage readers which takes a character from the present into a much earlier period. An unusually observant adolescent girl, Penelope Cameron, becomes so devoted to Thackers, the ancient family farmhouse to which she comes for a visit, that there isn't a stretch of its grounds or essential history which she fails to know and love. Incidents which take place there during the Tudor period and which bring to life the story of Mary, Queen of Scots, become as real to her as they were, in dreams, to Alison Uttley herself.

Improbably romantic as some of these incidents are, compared with those in later time travel fantasies written by others, the novel commands intense interest still.

Books for older readers (12 to 15 years)

FANTASY:
*Spiritual quests/
Spiritual warfare*

'You must not change one thing, one pebble, one grain of sand, until you know what good and evil will follow on that act.'

Ursula Le Guin, *A Wizard of Earthsea*

SINGLE NOVELS

☞ Annerton Pit

Peter Dickinson, Gollancz, 1977 (England). Ages 12-14 years. LIBRARY, CHILD

Like all of Peter Dickinson's books, this one immerses readers in its world and raises mysterious questions requiring answers. The large, unresolved problem confronting blind, thirteen-year-old Jake and his older brother Martin at the start is why postcards from the north of England from their normally reliable grandfather have stopped coming.

In the absence of adult advice — their parents are in the Bahamas on a cornflakes packet win — Martin decides to take Jake north on his newly purchased motor bike to find Grandpa. Near Annerton Pit, the site of an eerie, perhaps supernaturally induced, 1830s mining disaster, they find their mother's father under conditions which strain their imaginative and physical resources to capacity.

Although, typically, Dickinson's plot has some far-fetched features, 'what happens next' always matters because his characters and their situations are made so real.

Other titles: *Tulku* (Carnegie Award, 1979), *The Blue Hawk* (Guardian Award, 1977) and others.

☞ *The Owl Service

Alan Garner, Lions, 1967 (England). Carnegie Medal, 1967; Guardian Award, 1968. Ages 14-15 years. LIBRARY, CHILD

Using a story from the *Mabinogion*, Alan Garner tells a fascinating, beautifully structured tale about three young people — Alison, Gwyn and Roger — who reproduce with frightening exactitude passions present

in their ancestors, but in a form suited to their own time and place. The central question posed by Garner is whether a centuries-old cycle of violence, engendered by pride and uncontrollable anger, can be broken and, if so, how. His answer, for readers who follow his subtle argument and its dramatic resolution with appropriate care, is deeply satisfying. There is a Christian dimension to it.

Other titles: *Elidor, Tom Fobble's Day* (see p. 68) and others.

☞ Michael and the Secret War

Cassandra Golds, Atheneum, 1985 (Australia). Ages 12-14 years. LIBRARY

Cassandra Golds is a gifted young Australian writer who thus far has produced one novel, written when she was nineteen. Its dialogue, its descriptions and its theme — secret spiritual warfare — reveal an unusual linguistic and personal outlook, and an attractive interest in large questions.

On its own, *Michael and the Secret War* has an unfinished feel. Michael's sensitivity to beings from different times — ghosts, saints, fairytale characters, and even different forms of life — engenders a series of fantastic adventures which puzzle, alarm, and thoroughly preoccupy him.

Golds' depiction of the war in which he is engaged is, at key points, too hazy and indirect to satisfy readers eager to enter his experience completely; but her delineation of his state of mind and his brief but telling encounters with extraordinary creatures is effective and promising.

☞ *The Magical Adventures of Pretty Pearl

Virginia Hamilton, Harper and Row, 1983 (USA). Ages 14-15 years. LIBRARY

Blending folklore from America and Africa with biblical notions, Virginia Hamilton has created a marvellous epic about a 'God' child named Pretty Pearl who steps down from Mount Kenya and enters the lives of a group of 'inside' folk who've broken loose from slavery's aftermath in a beautiful forest in Georgia. The vitality, lyricism, warmth and humour of her portraits of black people from myth, legend and her own imaginings, and the depth of her understanding of mortality, make the book a rarity.

Other titles: *Sweet Whispers, Brother Rush* (Newbery Award,1983), *M.C. Higgins the Great* (see p. 108) and many others.

☞ *Dogsbody

Diana Wynne Jones, Macmillan, 1975 (England). Ages 14-15 years. LIBRARY

Life on earth as it is experienced by a reborn dog named Leo who is really Sirius the Dog-Star, is the subject of Diana Wynne Jones' compelling fantasy. Leo's large task is to discover a murderous weapon called the Zoi, which has mysteriously found its way onto our planet; but he has no idea what this weapon looks like, let alone where it may be found.

As we enter his daily round and watch him coping with being a puppy, learning to understand English, defending his mistress Kathleen (an Irish girl living with an unappreciative and sometimes unwittingly brutal English family), getting on with other dogs, escaping undetected from his 'home' and making friends outside it, and moving closer to the source of the mystery it is his job to unravel, we become more and more deeply involved in his dreams and desires.

Other titles: *Charmed Life* (Guardian Award, 1978), *The Ogre Downstairs* and many other (often amusing) fantasies.

☞ The Changeover

Margaret Mahy, Magnet, 1984 (NZ). Carnegie Medal, 1984. Ages 13-15 years. LIBRARY, CHILD, GENERAL

The line between books which dabble dangerously in the occult and those which depict worrying supernatural events in acceptable though non-religious terms is sometimes difficult to draw. I found this book borderline, and for that reason was uneasy about the struggles of its heroine, Laura, with the demonic Carmody Braque, who preys on her younger brother. Laura's developing relationships with a highly imaginative and unconventional young man named Sorenson Carlisle, her mother Kate and Kate's boyfriend Chris are developed in a more clear-cut and untroubling way.

Other titles: *Alien in the Family, Memory* (see p. 114) and many others.

☞ Space Demons
Gillian Rubinstein, Omnibus-Puffin, 1986 (England).
Ages 12-14 years. LIBRARY, CHILD, GENERAL

This is the most inventive of Gillian Rubinstein's tales about the effects of sinister threats — both physical and emotional — upon resourceful children. It recounts the dangers confronting an egotistical young man named Andrew Hayford when he enters the world of a computer game which he plays obsessively. The most important discovery he makes is that he cannot survive in space without the aid of two other adolescents whose lives are imperilled because of his selfishness.

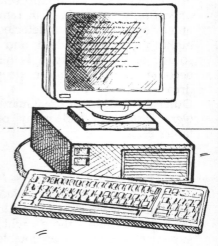

Rubinstein is interesting, though not entirely convincing, on what is required to change Andrew. Her prose is flash and too often clichéd; but her narrative skills are compelling, and effectively address reluctant readers.

Other titles: There's a troubling degree of hostility and brutality in Rubinstein's novels for older children — including this book's sequel, *Skymaze*, and the popular *Answers to Brut*.

☞ *Child of the Owl

> *Laurence Yep, Dell, 1977 (Chinese-USA). Globe/Horn Book Award, 1977. Ages 12-15 years.* LIBRARY

Life in San Francisco's Chinatown with Paw-Paw, the maternal grandmother with whom Casey stays when her down-and-out father is in hospital, is unpredictably rich. Surrounded for the first time by Chinese people, introduced to fascinating snippets of family history and legend and slowly given access to essential knowledge about herself and her parents, she discovers her place in the world.

Laurence Yep involves readers deeply in the worlds Casey discovers, especially the one inhabited by Paw-Paw. With quiet felicity he reveals the connections between legend and apparently mundane reality, filial piety and personal growth, uncomplaining perseverance and true purpose.

Other titles: *Dragonwings* (Newbery Honor Book), *Sweetwater* and others.

SERIES

☞ *The High King

> *Lloyd Alexander, Dell Yearling, 1968 (USA). Newbery Award, 1969. Ages 12-15 years.* LIBRARY, CHILD

In *The High King*, Fflewddur the harpist announces, 'I've rescued more captives than I have fingers on my hands' and then, hearing his harp shudder, he admits, 'Planned to rescue, that is.' In their calmer moments, Lloyd Alexander's most attractive characters share Fflewddur's humour, charm and unheroic candour. When pressed, however, they sound more like the large figures we've come to expect in fantasies which depict great cosmic battles between good and evil.

Whether danger is imminent, present or distant in Prydain, the world created by Alexander from Welsh and Celtic myth and his own imagining inspires strong interest. Its talking animals — Kaw the crow, Hen Wen the pig — its dwarf Doli, its magician Dallben, its hero Taran the Assistant Pig-Keeper, its villain Arawn-Death-Lord and a host of other characters are vividly drawn. Slow patches in the narrative are succeeded by events so startling — a harp playing all night, a young man carried by a bird — that we see them all in appropriate perspective.

Other titles: *The Book of Three, The Black Cauldron, The Castle of Llyr* and *Taran Wanderer.*

☞ *The Dark Is Rising

Susan Cooper, Puffin, 1973 (England). Globe/Horn Book Award, 1973. Ages 12-14 years.
LIBRARY, CHILD, GENERAL

The usual reaction of readers new to this engrossing series is to gobble up all five books as quickly as possible. Susan Cooper's central focus is the struggle that must take place between a group of characters called the Old Ones, who represent the forces of light on earth, and their enemies, who represent darkness.

In *The Dark Is Rising*, the second book in the sequence, Cooper's central character, Will Stanton, a boy who is also an Old One, must overcome horrifying threats to England with the help of a figure from *Over Sea, Under Stone*, Merriman, and other very attractive helpmates of his.

As in all of the novels in the series, untrustworthy characters can be recognised by their behaviour in the everyday world, as well as by their more obviously destructive actions in the world of fantasy. Scenes of brilliant evocativeness dramatise key struggles.

Other titles: *The Grey King* (Newbery Award, 1976, Globe/Horn Book Award, 1977), *Greenwitch, Silver on the Tree* and *Over Sea, Under Stone.*

☞ Dragons in the Waters

Madeleine L'Engle, Dell, 1976 (USA). Ages 12-15 years.
LIBRARY, CHILD and some Christian bookshops.

This is the first of a series of a books in which Poly and Charles O'Keefe, the children of Meg and Calvin (see the *Ring of Endless Light*), figure prominently. Its intricate, not entirely credible plot centres around the theft of a painting which assumes a crucial role in a cosmic struggle between the forces of good and evil. Canon Tom Tallis, the middle-aged clergyman who plays an important role in L'Engle's novels about the Austins, also appears in this book.

Companion Books: *The Arms of the Starfish* and *A House Like a Lotus.*

Other series: *A Ring of Endless Light* (see p. 119) and *A Wind in the Door* (see p. 94).

☞ *A Wizard of Earthsea

Ursula Le Guin, Puffin, 1968 (USA) Ages 12-14 years.
LIBRARY, CHILD, GENERAL

On the island of Roke in the Northeast Sea, a boy named Sparrowhawk (Ged) is trained to be a wizard. Before he is properly equipped to deal with the mighty powers of his trade, in an angry response to a boy studying with him, he tempts these powers and unleashes a beast called the Shadow. Most of the novel is concerned with the kinds of painful experience he must have in order to kill this beast — his own pride — and become a proper mage. Chiefly, he discovers what he cannot do, much as he would wish to do it.

Le Guin is masterful on the spiritual trials Ged undergoes and the connection between spiritual and imaginative maturity, though her approach is not explicitly religious. She is also very interesting on the nature and power of art.

Other titles: *The Tombs of Atuan*, *The Farthest Shore* (National Book Award) and *Tehanu* (recently published).

☞ *The Hero and the Crown

Robin McKinley, Morrow, 1984 (USA). Newbery Medal, 1985. Ages 13-15 years. LIBRARY

The quest of Aerin, the daughter of Arlbeth, King of Damar, is the subject of this fascinating book to which her acclaimed *Blue Sword* is a sequel. To get to the bottom of mysteries surrounding her long-deceased mother (Was she a witch? What was the nature of her gift?), and also to recapture the hero's crown which ensures Damar's power but is temporarily in the hands of an evil mage, Agsded, Aerin must endure arduous trials. Among them are a series of battles with dragons — battles so imaginatively conceived that others in children's fiction appear almost drab by comparison.

The entire novel, in fact, is a marvel: so good conceptually and in its handling of key events that its more ponderous bits can be forgiven. On mortality, it is especially provocative.

Other titles in the series: So far in Australia, *The Blue Sword*.

Appendix

Prizes for fiction written in the last thirty years

AUSTRALIAN CHILDREN'S BOOK AWARDS

1958	Nan Chauncy	Tiger in the Bush	Oxford
1959	Nan Chauncy	Devil's Hill	Oxford
	John Gunn	Sea Menace	Constable
1960	Kylie Tennant	All the Proud Tribesmen	Macmillan
1961	Nan Chauncy	Tangara	Oxford
1962	H.L. Evers	The Racketty Street Gang	Hodder
	Joan Woodbery	Rafferty Rides a Winner	Parrish
1963	Joan Phipson	The Family Conspiracy	A & R
1964	Eleanor Spence	The Green Laurel	Oxford
1965	Hesba Brinsmead	Pastures of the Blue Crane	Oxford, Puffin
1966	Ivan Southall	Ash Road	A & R, Puffin
1967	Mavis Thorpe Clark	The Min Min	Landsdowne
1968	Ivan Southall	To the Wild Sky	Puffin
1969	Margaret Balderson	When Jays Fly to Barbmo	Oxford
1970	Annette Macarthur-Onslow	Uhu	Ure Smith
1971	Ivan Southall	Bread and Honey	A & R, Puffin
1972	Hesba Brinsmead	Longtime Passing	A & R, Puffin
1973	Noreen Shelly	Family at the Lookout	Oxford
1974	Patricia Wrightson	The Nargun and the Stars	Hutchinson, Puffin
1975	No award.		
1976	Ivan Southall	Fly West	A & R, Puffin
1977	Eleanor Spence	The October Child	Oxford
1978	Patricia Wrightson	The Ice is Coming	Hutchinson
1979	Ruth Manley	The Plum Rain Scroll	Hodder, Knight
1980	Lee Harding	Displaced Person	Hyland House, Puffin
1981	Ruth Park	Playing Beatie Bow	Nelson, Puffin
1982	Colin Thiele	Valley Between	Rigby

1983	Victor Kelleher	Master of the Grove	Penguin
1984	Patricia Wrightson	A Little Fear	Hutchinson, Penguin
1985	James Aldridge	The True Story of Lilli Stubeck	Penguin
1986	Thurley Fowler	The Green Wind	Dent
1987	Simon French	All We Know	A & R
1988	John Marsden	So Much to Tell You	McVitty
1989	Gillian Rubinstein	Beyond the Labyrinth	Hyland House
1990	Robin Klein	Came Back to Show You I Could Fly	Viking Kestrel
1991	Gary Crews	Strange Objects	Heinemann

AUSTRALIAN MEDAL FOR JUNIOR READERS
This award was initiated in 1982.

1982	Christobel Mattingley	Rummage	A & R
1983	Robin Klein	Thing	Oxford
1984	Max Dann	Bernice Knows Best	Oxford
1985	Emily Rodda	Something Special	A & R
1986	Mary Steele	Arkwright	Hyland House, Nelson
1987	Emily Rodda	Pigs Might Fly	A & R
1988	Nadia Wheatley	My Place	Collins
1989	Emily Rodda	The Best-Kept Secret	A & R
1990	Jeanie Adams	Pigs and Honey	Omnibus
1991	Emily Rodda	Finders Keepers	Omnibus

CARNEGIE MEDAL (Great Britain)

1958	Philippa Pearce	Tom's Midnight Garden	Oxford
1959	Rosemary Sutcliff	The Lantern Bearers	Oxford
1960	I.W. Cornwall	The Making of Man	Phoenix House
1961	Lucy Boston	A Stranger at Green Knowe	Faber
1962	Pauline Clarke	The Twelve and the Genii	Faber
1963	Hester Burton	Time of Trial	Oxford
1964	Sheena Porter	Nordy Bank	Oxford
1965	Philip Turner	The Grange at High Force	Oxford
1966	No award		
1967	Alan Garner	The Owl Service	Collins
1968	Rosemary Harris	The Moon in the Cloud	Faber
1969	K.M. Peyton	The Edge of the Cloud	Oxford
1970	Garfield & Blishen	The God Beneath the Sea	Kestrel
1971	Ivan Southall	Josh	A & R
1972	Richard Adams	Watership Down	Rex Collings
1973	Penelope Lively	The Ghost of Thomas Kemp	Heinemann
1974	Mollie Hunter	The Stronghold	Hamilton
1975	Robert Westall	The Machine-Gunners	Macmillan
1976	Jan Mark	Thunder and Lightnings	Kestrel
1977	Gene Kemp	The Turbulent Term of Tyke Tiler	Faber

1978	David Rees	Exeter Blitz	Hamilton
1979	Peter Dickinson	Tulka	Gollancz
1980	Peter Dickinson	City of Gold	Gollancz
1981	Robert Westall	The Scarecrows	Chatto & Windus
1982	Margaret Mahy	The Haunting	Dent
1983	Jan Mark	Handles	Kestrel
1984	Margaret Mahy	The Changeover	Dent
1985	Kevin Crossley-Holland	Storm	Heinemann
1986	Berlie Doherty	Granny Was a Buffer Girl	Methuen
1987	Susan Price	The Ghost Drum	Faber
1988	Geraldine McCaughrean	A Pack of Lies	Oxford
1989	Anne Fine	My War with Goggle-Eyes	Hamilton

GUARDIAN AWARD (Great Britain)
This award was begun in 1967.

1967	Leon Garfield	Devil in the Fog	Longman
1968	Alan Garner	The Owl Service	Collins
1969	Joan Aiken	The Whispering Mountain	Jonathan Cape
1970	K.M. Peyton	Flambards (The Trilogy)	Oxford
1971	John Christopher	The Guardians	Hamish Hamilton
1972	Gillian Avery	A Likely Lad	Collins
1973	Richard Adams	Watership Down	Collins
1974	Barbara Willard	The Iron Lily	Longman Young
1975	Winifred Cawley	Gran at Coalgate	Oxford
1976	Nina Bawden	Peppermint Pig	Gollancz
1977	Peter Dickinson	The Blue Hawk	Gollancz
1978	Diana Wynne Jones	Charmed Life	Macmillan
1979	Andrew Davies	Conrad's War	Blackie
	Ann Schlee	The Vandal	Macmillan
1980	Peter Carter	The Sentinels	Oxford
1981	Robert Westall	The Scarecrows	Chatto & Windus
1982	Michelle Magorian	Goodnight Mister Tom	Kestrel
1983	Anita Desai	The Village By the Sea	Heinemann
1984	Dick King-Smith	The Sheep-Pig	Gollancz
1985	Ted Hughes	What is the Truth?	Faber
1986	Ann Pilling	Henry's Leg	Kestrel
1987	James Aldridge	The True Story of Spit MacPhee	Kestrel
1988	Ruth Thomas	The Runaways	Hutchinson
1989	Geraldine McCaughrean	A Pack of Lies	Oxford
1990	Anne Fine	My War with Goggle-Eyes	Hamilton
1991	Robert Westall	Kingdom by the Sea	Octopus

NEWBERY AWARD (United States)

| 1958 | Harold Keith | Rifles for Watie | Crowell |

1959	Elizabeth George Speare	The Witch of Blackbird Pond	Houghton
1960	Joseph Krumgold	Onion John	Crowell
1961	Scott O'Dell	Island of the Blue Dolphins	Houghton
1962	Elizabeth George Speare	The Bronze Bow	Houghton
1963	Madeleine L'Engle	A Wrinkle in Time	Farrar
1964	Emily Neville	It's Like This, Cat	Harper
1965	Maia Wojciechowska	Shadow of a Bull	Atheneum
1966	Elizabeth Borten de Trevino	I, Juan de Pareja	Farrar
1967	Irene Hunt	Up a Road Slowly	Follett
1968	E.L. Konigsburg	From the Mixed-up Files of Mrs Basil E. Frankweiler	Atheneum
1969	Lloyd Alexander	The High King	Holt
1970	William H. Armstrong	Sounder	Harper
1971	Betsy Byars	Summer of the Swans	Viking
1972	Robert C. O'Brien	Mrs Frisby and the Rats of NIMH	Atheneum
1973	Jean Craighead George	Julie of the Wolves	Harper
1974	Paula Fox	The Slave Dancer	Bradbury
1975	Virginia Hamilton	M.C. Higgins the Great	Macmillan
1976	Susan Cooper	The Grey King	McElderry/ Atheneum
1977	Mildred Taylor	Roll of Thunder, Hear My Cry	Dial
1978	Katherine Paterson	Bridge to Terabithia	Crowell
1979	Ellen Raskin	The Westing Game	Dutton
1980	Joan M. Blos	A Gathering of Days	Scribner
1981	Katherine Paterson	Jacob Have I Loved	Crowell
1982	Nancy Willard	A Visit to William Blake's Inn	Harcourt
1983	Cynthia Voigt	Dicey's Song	Atheneum
1984	Beverly Cleary	Dear Mr Henshaw	Morrow
1985	Robin McKinley	The Hero and the Crown	MacRae
1986	Patricia MacLachlan	Sarah, Plain and Tall	Harper
1987	Sid Fleischman	The Whipping Boy	Morrow
1988	Russell Friedman	Lincoln: A Photobiography	Clarion/ Houghton
1989	Paul Fleischman	Joyful Noise: Poems for Two Voices	Harper
1990	Lois Lowry	Number the Stars	Houghton Mifflin
1991	Jerry Spinelli	Maniac Magee	Little Brown

NATIONAL BOOK AWARD (United States)

| 1969 | Meindert DeJong | Journey from Peppermint Street | Harper |
| 1970 | I.B. Singer | A Day of Pleasure: Stories of a Boy Growing Up | Farrar |

1971	Lloyd Alexander	The Marvellous Misadventures of Sebastian	Dutton
1972	Donald Barthelme	The Slightly Irregular Fire Engine	Farrar
1973	Ursula Le Guin	The Farthest Shore	Atheneum
1974	Eleanor Cameron	The Court of the Stone Children	Dutton
1975	Virginia Hamilton	M.C. Higgins the Great	Macmillan
1976	Walter Edmonds	Bert Breen's Barn	Little
1977	Katherine Paterson	The Master Puppeteer	Crowell
1978	Judith and Herbert Kohl	The View from the Oak	Scribner
1979	Katherine Paterson	The Great Gilly Hopkins	Crowell

AMERICAN BOOK AWARD (United States)
Formerly the National Book Award.

1980	Joan Blos	A Gathering of Days	Scribner
1981	Betsy Byars	The Night Swimmers	Delacorte
1982	Lloyd Alexander	Westmark	Dutton
1983	Jean Fritz	Homesick: My Own Story	Putnam

This award was then discontinued.

BOSTON GLOBE/HORN BOOK AWARDS (United States)
These awards were begun in 1967.

1968	John Lawson	The Spring Rider	Rowell
1969	Ursula Le Guin	A Wizard of Earthsea	Parnassus
1970	John Rowe Townsend	The Intruder	Lippincott
1971	Eleanor Cameron	A Room Made of Windows	Little Brown
1972	Rosemary Sutcliff	Tristan and Iseult	Dutton
1973	Susan Cooper	The Dark is Rising	Atheneum
1974	Virginia Hamilton	M.C. Higgins the Great	Macmillan
1975	T. Degens	Transport 7-41-R	Viking
1976	Jill Paton Walsh	Unleaving	Farrar
1977	Laurence Yep	Child of the Owl	Harper & Row
1978	Ellen Raskin	The Westing Game	Dutton
1979	Sid Fleischman	Humbug Mountain	Little Brown
1980	Andrew Davies	Conrad's War	Crown
1981	Lynn Hall	The Leaving	Scribner
1982	Ruth Park	Playing Beatie Bow	Atheneum
1983	Virginia Hamilton	Sweet Whispers, Brother Rush	Philomel
1984	Patricia Wrightson	A Little Fear	Atheneum
1985	Bruce Brooks	The Moves Make the Man	Harper & Row
1986	Zibby Oneal	In Summer Light	Viking
1987	Lois Lowry	Rabble Starkey	Houghton Mifflin
1988	Mildred D. Taylor	The Friendship	Dial
1989	Paula Fox	The Village by the Sea	Orchard
1990	Jerry Spinalli	Maniac Magee	Little Brown

Index

Authors

Titles